| Science Fiction | EDITED BY Ben Bova | Writing Series |

Time Travel

Paul J. Nahin

WRITER'S DIGEST BOOKS
Cincinnati, Ohio

D0278981

01   00   99   98   97   5   4   3   2   1

Library of Congress Cataloging-in-Publication Data

Nahin, Paul J.
    Time travel / by Paul J. Nahin.
    Includes bibliographical references and index.
    ISBN 0-89879-748-9 (pbk.: alk. paper)
    1. Science fiction—Authorship.   2. Science fiction—History and
  criticism—Theory, etc.   3. Time travel in literature.   I. Title.
PN3377.5.S3N34   1997
808.3'8762—dc21   96-30080
                                                                  CIP

Edited by Ben Bova
Production edited by Kathleen Anne Brauer and Katie Carroll
Interior designed by Kathy DeZarn and Angela Lennert Wilcox
Cover designed by Angela Lennert Wilcox
Cover illustration by Bob Eggleton

Kurt Gödel (1906-1978) and Albert Einstein (1879-1955), the father and grandfather, respectively, of time travel based on science. Photo taken the year before Einstein's death, by Richard Arens at the Institute for Advanced Study, Princeton, New Jersey.

ABOUT THE AUTHOR

Paul J. Nahin is Professor of Electrical Engineering at the University of New Hampshire. He holds three engineering degrees from Stanford (BS), CalTech (MS), and the University of California at Irvine (PhD). Before beginning his academic teaching career more than twenty-five years ago, he spent over seven years in the Southern California aerospace industry as a digital systems designer, and later nearly three more years in Washington, DC as a military systems analyst for the Defense Department. He is the author of three other books: *Oliver Heaviside* (IEEE Press 1988), *Time Machines* (AIP Press 1993), and *The Science of Radio* (AIP Press 1995). His book *An Imaginary Tale*, on the history and applications of complex numbers, will be published by Princeton University Press in 1998. He has written technical non-fiction for *IEEE Spectrum* and *Scientific American* magazines, and his short-story science fiction has appeared in *Analog, Omni,* and *Twilight Zone* magazines, as well as in original book collections. He has appeared on National Public Radio's *Science Friday* program to discuss time travel, and has served as a technical consultant to BBC and Discovery Channel film makers on the subject.

ABOUT THE EDITOR

Ben Bova is the author of *Mars, Moonrise,* and more than ninety other novels, nonfiction and instructional books, including *The Craft of Writing Science Fiction That Sells* for Writer's Digest Books. He is also the co-author of the Science Fiction Writing Series book *Space Travel.* The former editor of *Analog Science Fiction* and *Omni* magazines, Bova is the six-time winner of science fiction's Hugo Award for Best Professional Editor. He is president emeritus of the National Space Society and a past president of Science Fiction and Fantasy Writers of America.

DEDICATION

For my two beautiful granddaughters Rebecca Danielle in Michigan and Courtney Anne in New Hampshire for whom I hope these words from Tennyson's "Locksley Hall," words that someday might be spoken by a time traveler, will prove to be prophetic: *For I dipt into the future, far as human eye could see, Saw the Vision of the world, and all the wonder that would be.*

ACKNOWLEDGEMENTS

I recall once reading the opening of a book written by a well known science fiction writer who, in effect, declared he was dedicating it to himself because he was the only one responsible for it. Some might find that a little silly, but not me because anybody who has written a book, and has lived with the "pain" that comes with that experience, understands an author's reluctance to share whatever pleasure may also result. I can't follow that author's example here, however, because while I alone wrote this book, it still simply would not have happened without Ben Bova. Ben bought my first science fiction tale back in 1977, and my first time travel story in 1979, when he was editor of *Analog.* When he moved on to become the first fiction editor at *Omni,* and later executive editor, he continued to buy my stories and articles. Now, as one of the best-known presences in the science fiction world, a man with world-wide literary connections, Ben could have asked any one of many people to write this book as part of the Writer's Digest Books science fiction series. The fact that he asked me was enormously flattering, and one that explains why I simply *have* to say, why I *must* and *want* to say, in appreciation for all that he has done for me over the last twenty years:

Thanks, Ben!

Also, my secretary Kimberly Riley prepared the computer code for all of the line illustrations, and David Borcherding, Kathleen Brauer, Katie Carroll and Kristin Earhart at Writer's Digest Books carefully read through the entire typescript and made a number of very helpful suggestions. To each thank you.

TABLE OF CONTENTS

WHAT THIS BOOK IS NOT ABOUT

Joey had no more Twilight Zone explanations to fall back upon, no more quirks of quantum physics, no more Star Trek time warps or energy waves . . . There was only the real thing now, the foul and ancient thing, purest evil . . . shrieking hatred, reeking of sulphur, dark devourer of souls, eater of hope. . . .

—thoughts of a man who has traveled twenty years back in time and who believes more in the supernatural than in science; from Dean Koontz's 1995 novella *Strange Highways*

INTRODUCTION

It is so full of invention and the invention is so wonderful . . .
it must certainly make your reputation.

from an 1894 letter by the editor of the *New Review*
to H.G. Wells, commenting on the not-yet-published
The Time Machine.

"The *science* of time travel?" you ask with a smile. I've got to be kidding, right? Everybody knows time travel is impossible because of something called *paradox* (something or other about killing your grandfather—or is it your nephew—before he has had a chance to create your mom or dad). Oh, sure, you'll admit that maybe you can travel into the future if you zip around the cosmos in a very fast rocketship. (Didn't Einstein prove that? Or maybe you saw it on TV's *Nova*.) Nevertheless, if you're honest you'll admit that even if Einstein did say that was OK, it still sounds pretty odd. But *no way*, you'll insist, could anyone travel into the *past*.

Probably every physicist alive would have agreed with you on this issue twenty-five years ago. Here's what one wrote, for example, in a 1971 issue of the scholarly journal *Studium Generale* (David Park, "The Myth of the Passage of Time"):

> Let us consider time travel in the manner of H.G. Wells. Suppose that I were really to travel in time back to my fifth birthday. Here are some children sitting around a table. I am five years old and know nothing of the time machine in my future. *If I really go back, then all traces of my intervening years, inside and outside me, are gone.*

(The italics are my emphasis. How this logic works escapes me, and Professor Park offers no explanation.)

> There is nothing remarkable about the birthday party. It is indistinguishable from the original one; in fact, it *is* the original

one. There are no consequences to time travel. A statement that time travel can, or cannot, or does, or does not take place is unverifiable and therefore, in my logic as a physicist, meaningless. What is usually called time travel should be called lack of time travel; Wells's picture is that I take my present mind back to past events. This I take to be fiction.

Up until recent years even the most speculative, wild-eyed physicist would have agreed with this skeptical reaction (one, I will claim as we go through this book, that has no connection at all with physics). The only place you could find people writing positively about time travel and time machines was in science fiction, and even science fiction writers didn't really believe the concept was anything more than a fantasy. They wrote time travel stories because readers loved the idea, and editors would pay for what the writers produced; but that didn't mean time travel might actually be possible. This was in distinct contrast to, for example, stories about space travel. Traveling to the moon, or Mars or even the nearest star would clearly be a very big engineering job, but it would violate no known laws of physics.

But *time travel?* No, that was just nonsense, fairy tale stuff. But now it's time to reevaluate. The real world is starting to look more like science fiction than the science fiction pulps ever did. Once, "computer brains" existed only on the pages of the pulps; now every other high school kid in America has one in the bedroom connecting him or her to the Internet. Once, trips into space were ridiculed as simply escapist twaddle, but now the space shuttle rumbles up to orbit and back on a regular schedule (and each time gets maybe thirty seconds of notice on CNN). And, once, talk of time travel was pretty far out even for science fiction, but now the theory of time machines is regular fare in the most important physics journals, in articles by some of the very best physicists in the world.

Today, a writer of science fiction who wants to use high-tech stuff like computers or space travel in a story has to constantly keep in mind that modern readers are not the teenage boys of the 1930s that kept *Thrilling Wonder Stories* and *Amazing Stories* in business. Today's readers know all about (or at least think they know all about) computer operating systems, high-speed electronics, Newton's laws of motion, the biochemistry of DNA, and certainly that a light-year is a measure of distance, not time. A modern writer of science fiction has to keep the science straight or, if the science *is* bent, at least give the reader reason to believe the bend is there for a reason and not just because the writer is ignorant. That cautionary flag is now up for writers of time travel, too.

Here's why. Physics seems to be coming to the astonishing conclusion that time travel to the past doesn't violate any of the known laws of physics. Nobody knows how to do it (yet) by using only the spare parts left over from the last time the vacuum cleaner was repaired; nevertheless, it looks as though time travel just might be possible someday, *with* sufficiently advanced technology. *Technology* is the key word here, not science. The current *science* says that time travel to the past is OK. But there are rules to time travel, based on the science. As a writer, you'll want to get these rules straight in your stories.

THE "LAWS" OF TIME TRAVEL

Up until a few years ago it was OK to simply make up your own rules for time travel. After all, who could say you were wrong? This was done, for example, by two English teachers writing in *Extrapolation,* an important journal of science fiction criticism. In "The Laws of Time Travel," S.J. Jakiel and R.E. Levinthal wrote (in the Summer 1980 issue) that their attempt at formulating time travel rules "gave us many hours of pleasant effort"; indeed, their essay *is* interesting reading. A great book that also plays pretty fast and loose with time travel is Dean Koontz's 1988 novel *Lightning.* Koontz's time traveler can change his own future (later in this book I'll take the position that this has no logical meaning), but not his own past. It doesn't matter that the past *is* changed for someone else living in the traveler's future. If you're Dean Koontz, you can get away with this sort of stuff (the book sold hugely), but it simply isn't logical.

Since 1988, much of the real science of time travel has been discovered by physicists, and the made-up "rules" of yesteryear are no longer even a passable guide to prospective science fiction writers. As you get further into this book you'll come to understand more and more the constraints that science imposes on an unbridled imagination. You'll also learn that these constraints, or "rules," are not really all that hard to live with. To be brief and unmysterious about this, let me just tell you for now that these rules boil down to two central ideas: (1) if your story has a single time track or line, the events around a closed loop in time must be consistent; e.g., you can't have a time traveler changing the past (although he or she can *affect* the past, and you'll see there is a difference), and (2) if your story does depend on changing the past, you must also introduce multiple time tracks, as with splitting universes. Rather than limiting you, these two central rules should actually encourage you to think more carefully about what you write, and so result in better stories.

This book will bring you up to date on what you need to know to write good science fiction time travel tales. Reading this book won't make you into a physicist, but when you're done, you should be able to make your treatments of time travel scientifically respectable (or at least *sound* that way). If you're not interested in scientific respectability, that's OK too; but be alert to the fact that knowledgeable readers, who may in fact greatly *enjoy* your work, will regard it as fantasy, not science fiction. As a writer you should know the difference (if only to know what to send to editors who are looking for science fiction but not fantasy, and vice versa).

To be honest, the distinction between fantasy and science fiction can be a fine one. In this book, however, I'll be concerned *only* with time travel in machines based on Einstein's general theory of relativity. (As I'll show you later, this will eliminate the most famous of all time machines, the so-called "Wellsian" time machine in *The Time Machine*.) The reason is simple—it's the *only* scientific theory we've got for time travel. Let me emphasize, again, that this is a bias based strictly on logical concerns. When it comes to simply telling a good story, however, what I call "fantasy" can nonetheless be enormously powerful. Let me give you one really outstanding example of it.

In the very clever (and very romantic) fantasy "Clap Hands and Sing" by Orson Scott Card (which can be found in his 1990 collection *Maps in a Mirror*), the inventor of "mind travel" uses it, as an old man, to travel back to *his own mind* in the past so he can make love to the young girl he passed over in his youth. (Ah, *the* ultimate male fantasy.) At the end of the story we learn that she, too, as an old woman, has traveled back to *her* mind, on the same day, to make love to *him*. There is no *science* in Card's story at all, really, but who can deny its tremendous appeal in addressing a fundamental aspect of the human condition?

OUTLINE OF THE BOOK

After a little historical development of fictional time travel in H.G. Wells's classic novella *The Time Machine* (1895), and in the pulps of the 1920s and 1930s, we will tackle the *science* of time travel. The physical ideas behind the science, and how they have been both used and abused by writers (and in the movies, too), will be presented. We'll get into time dilation, space-time (both flat and curved), world lines, the fourth dimension, the direction of time (and how we distinguish past from future) and time travel in universes that rotate. For our discussion of Einstein's general theory of relativity—his theory of gravity, which *is* the theory of time travel—there are two or three instances of simple mathematical expressions, all of which have actually appeared in published stories.

I'll also discuss the idea of antimatter as particles traveling backward in time, as well as the lesser known theory from classical physics that seems to allow sending radio messages into the past. We'll get into the theory and fiction of time machine inventions, such as infinite rotating cylinders, wormholes and cosmic strings. Along the way we'll run into Cauchy and chronology horizons, faster-than-light tachyons, black holes, causal loops and the sexual paradoxes (could you *really* be your own ancestor?), and the metaphysical quicksand of free will.

And after all *that* we'll head on into quantum mechanics combined with general relativity to get quantum gravity, and how
Stephen Hawking (who *hates* time travel theories) believes quantum
gravity will, ultimately, *prevent* it. You'll also see how some of
Hawking's colleagues think he is wrong (which is good, because
that means you can write time travel stories and still call them science fiction). I'll discuss how these ideas have been used—and often
mangled—in published stories. That is what we are going to do.

The reason for going through all this work is nicely summed up
in an exchange between two characters in the story "The Garden"
by G. Gor. In that tale a time traveler, born in 2003, turns up in 1975
and tries to convince an interrogator that the traveler won't be born
for another twenty-eight years. And apparently he does, as the time
traveler later tells a new friend in the past, "What amazed me . . .
was that he really believed me in the end." But the friend doesn't
buy it, replying "He did? I think he just pretended. A scientist isn't
likely to believe a thing that is against all logic." And neither will
the readers of your stories, unless you give them some help.

A time travel story is always a *lot* more convincing as science
fiction if some sort of scientific explanation for time travel is offered
to the reader. The time traveling tourist stranded in the past, in Joe
Haldeman's "No Future In It," for example, is used to a skeptical
reaction because he can provide no explanation for his situation.
When asked how time machines work, he can only reply "How the
hell should I know? I'm just a tourist. It has something to do with
chronons. Temporal Uncertainty Principle. Conservation of coincidence. I'm no engineer." Reading this book won't make you into an
engineer, either, but it *can* help you to sound like one when it's time
for a little tech talk in your stories.

It is remarkable that it wasn't until relatively recent times that
writers of science-oriented tales came to realize the importance of
technical verisimilitude. In 1934, in the preface to a collection of
his scientific romances (*Seven Famous Novels*, Knopf), H.G. Wells
explained how *he* came to realize this: "These stories of mine col-
lected here do not pretend to deal with possible things; they are

exercises of the imagination. . . . They are all fantasies, they do not aim to project a serious possibility; they aim indeed only at the same amount of conviction as one gets in a good gripping dream." Wells then went on to write that all previous attempts at writing fantastic stories depended on magic. But not his. "It occurred to me that instead of the usual interview with the devil or a magician, an ingenious use of scientific patter might with advantage be substituted." Indeed, in *The Time Machine* the fourth dimension is simply a "magic trick for a glimpse of the future."

Still, even after Wells, the Devil has not quite disappeared from time travel. For example, in mystery writer John Dickson Carr's 1951 novel *The Devil in Velvet* we find a professor of history at Cambridge University traveling back from 1925 to 1675, with the Devil's aid, in an attempt to prevent a murder he has read about in an ancient manuscript. (I discuss other, post-Wells "devilish" time travel tales in my book *Time Machines*.)

It was, perhaps, this unhappiness with the "magic" of time travel that prompted the following, an excerpt I've taken from a letter written by a seventeen year old and published in the December 1931 issue of *Astounding Stories*:

> There is only one kind of Science Fiction story that I dislike, and that is the so-called time-traveling. It doesn't seem logical to me. For example: supposing a man had a grudge against his grandfather, who is now dead. He could hop in his machine and go back to the year that his grandfather was a young man and murder him. And if he did this how could the revenger be born? I think the whole thing is the "bunk."

The skepticism expressed by this reader is still very much alive. Modern science fiction writer Orson Scott Card, for example, echoed this sentiment in 1990 in his collection *Maps in a Mirror*, when he wrote of time travel as an impossibility, calling time machines simply a "magic trick" for writers of fiction. As a writer you want feelings of excitement, tension and an eagerness to turn the page from your readers. Not raised eyebrows and skepticism at the very premise of your story. So, while you don't want to turn your tales into sleep-inducing doctoral dissertations in physics, you do want to provide *some* rationale for encouraging your readers to give your stories what every science fiction writer aims for—a willing, temporary "suspension of disbelief." That's what this book will help you do.

So, let's get to it.

CHAPTER 1

Time Travel in the Pulps

A time machine? Nonsense. A hilgeful of crap. Physical, mathematical, logical impossibility. I proved it once, for a term paper in the philosophy of science.

thoughts of Duncan Reid, a twentieth-century man,
as he begins to suspect the truth after a malfunction-
ing time machine has hurled him into the distant
past in Poul Anderson's 1972 novel *The Dancer From
Atlantis.*

In an editorial published in the November 1926 issue of *Amazing Stories* ("Plausibility in Scientifiction"), Hugo Gernsback wrote:

[E]ven in the best-written fiction stories you will notice the characters converse in rather extraordinary language. This is the so-called fiction language and is not generally used in real life. Open almost any first-class magazine and, if you stop to think a second, you will realize that human beings do not use the flowery language that the characters do in fiction. This same is true of scientifiction in another respect, where authors often take poetic license, sometimes disregarding true scientific facts, although still retaining enough scientific accuracy to make the plot or story seem probable and at the same time interesting.

I don't believe any good science fiction editor today would allow
a writer to ignore "true scientific facts" (with the exception of an
obvious spoof), and certainly no writer who hopes to sell his or her
work should believe it's OK to write dialogue in "fiction language."
One of the goals of this book is to help you tell your time-travel tales
without resorting to "fiction language."

Time machines and time travel are certainly radical topics that
demand a skeptical reaction. Even if physics should one day establish these topics on firm scientific and *experimental* grounds, I think
many people will persist in thinking of them as fantasy (just as physicists who understand the optical properties of water droplets still
stand in awe at the appearance of a rainbow). In 1979, the science
fiction grand master Lester del Rey wrote in his *The World of Science
Fiction: 1926–1976* that time travel is one of the genre's conventions
that "seems clearly impossible."

Del Rey's position was nothing new among science fiction critics,
because, as early as 1960, writer-critic Kingsley Amis wrote in *New
Maps of Hell* that "time travel is inconceivable." And even then the
view wasn't original, as in 1953, the respected anthologist Groff
Conklin wrote the following as an introduction to Murray Leinster's
time-travel story "The Middle of the Week After Next" (in *Science
Fiction Adventures in Dimension*): "In this tale we meet our first
Mad Scientist. Just as in reality the thoroughly cracked pots used
to be found inventing perpetual motion machines, so in science fiction we find the lunatic fringe more often than not trying to perfect
time-travel mechanisms."

And finally, as long ago as 1940 a writer in the British pulp *Tales
of Wonder* wrote words that many (but not all) physicists today might
agree with: "Of all the fantastic ideas that belong to science fiction,
the most remarkable—and, perhaps, the most fascinating—is that
of time travel . . . indeed, so fantastic a notion does it seem, and
so many apparently obvious absurdities and bewildering paradoxes
does it present, that some of the most imaginative students of science refuse to consider it as a practicable proposition . . ."

(An aside: See those words "obvious absurdities and bewildering paradoxes"? They are the doorway to fascinating stories, many already written but with *lots* more yet to be written. And that is the case, even if time machines and time travel prove to be truly impossible.)

And, in fact, who could honestly say that Conklin, Amis and del Rey weren't correct? After all, could there be a bigger fantasy than going back in time and having another try at putting muddled matters straight? The editor of the science fiction pulp *Thrilling Wonder Stories* knew the answer, and he used the powerful emotional hook of changing the past in this 1950 passage hyping a time-travel story coming in the next issue: "What's the biggest mistake you ever made? Don't worry about it. You may have pulled some awful boners in your time, but there's a sure-fire remedy for them all. It's simple. Just look up at that old time-clock on the wall—and turn it back to the moment just preceding your terrible blunder. Then make your corrections—and set your time-clock back to the present. You may be starting a new chain of error, but why fret? You can go back in time again. . . ." As you can see from those words, the concept behind the 1993 fantasy loop-in-time film *Groundhog Day* is nothing new (in fact, it appeared in the pulps long before 1950).

In the Introduction, I gave one example of good fantasy time travel, and because the distinction between fantasy and *scientific* time travel is so important, I want to elaborate on this point a bit more.

Consider how one author was able to take the idea of *mind travel*, a fantasy interpretation of time travel without any scientific support (as in TV's *Quantum Leap*) and, with a clever bit of "explanation," make it *seem* reasonable. In this tale ("Terror Out of Time," *Astounding Stories*, December 1933) the young writer Jack Williamson (who is still writing today) has a gadget-nutty professor tell us that he has discovered "a [magnetic current] that enables me to warp space-time along the time dimension . . . it enables me to bring the brain of my subject, in the present, into very intimate contact with the brain of some other human being, perhaps a million years distant in time, or a hundred million. They are brought together, so to speak, by bending the time dimension." Then the professor explains that thoughts can be transferred between the two brains by a process called "neuroinduction," an effect apparently much like putting your kitchen radio too close to the microwave induces a 60-cycle AC hum from the cooker's power transformer into the loud-speaker. Williamson's professor would, today, be considered a goofy, stereotypical character, unsuitable for any story other than a spoof, but the scientific explanation offered for mind travel is (and I write as an electrical engineering professor) not bad, not bad at all.

Other explanations for time travel that are pure fantasy are easier to spot, as in Edith Nesbit's description of a magical trip into the past in her 1907 novel *The Story of the Amulet*, and in Maurice Maeterlink's 1908 play *The Blue Bird* (in which a fairy sends two children on a search through time to find the blue bird of happiness). Other fantasy mechanisms for time travel include willpower (Richard Matheson's *Bid Time Return*, made into the romantic 1980 film *Somewhere in Time*, and Jack Finney's *Time and Again* and its sequel *From Time To Time*) and freezing (William Clark Russell's 1887 novel *The Frozen Pirate*, and the first part of Robert Heinlein's 1956 classic *The Door Into Summer*).

In contrast to these excellent uses of time travel fantasy, there are some just plain dumb time travel fantasy ideas that I hope you'll never be tempted to use. Consider one tale that made a fool out of the author (to say nothing of the editor who bought it): N. Loomis's "The Long Dawn," published in a 1950 issue of *Super Science Stories*. This story is simply stuffed with scientific nonsense, not the least of which is the arrival of a prehistoric nuclear physicist and his two telepathic pets (a pterodactyl and a tyrannosaur) in modern times. The trio finds itself in the twentieth century via a drug-induced snooze in a vault for one hundred million years. Oh, please! The idea of "sleeping into the future" was OK for Sleeping Beauty and Rip Van Winkle, and it created good adult fiction *in 1771*, in Mercier's *L'An Deux Mille Quatre Cent Quarante*. Later, Bellamy's 1888 *Looking Backward* was a huge hit with its hero sleeping to the year 2000, but by the time Buck Rogers used it to get into the twenty-fifth century it was already a cliché. It is now a dead and really cold idea, and any story that uses sleeping to get a character into the far future (as opposed to using a routine coma to simply get a character into next year) will automatically fail. Don't use it.

And by the way, sleeping to get into the past is old hat, too. William Morris used it for perhaps its last justifiable time in his *A Dream of John Ball* (serialized in *The Commonweal* in 1886–1887). Morris's hero finds the Middle Ages a nice place to wake up (which is hard for anyone who reads history to believe) after falling asleep in the nineteenth century. This story is simply an exercise in romantic nostalgia, not science fiction. Feminist writer Katharine Burdekin used this gimmick in her 1934 British novel of social criticism, *Proud Man*, to get a character from the far future into "our" times. As social criticism, it was well-received; science fiction (which Burdekin probably hadn't even heard of in 1934), it simply isn't.

A particularly silly time travel mechanism, in my opinion, is trauma. Mark Twain makes it work in *A Connecticut Yankee in King Arthur's Court*, yes, but that's because he doesn't make a big deal out of it—simply a knock on the head at the beginning and hardly a specific mention of time travel again. Trauma-induced time travel has even appeared in a silent movie: in the 1925 *The Road to Yesterday*, based on the 1907 New York stage play of the same name, five people are hurled into the distant past when they are involved in a spectacular train crash. Octavia Butler uses a related approach in her 1979 novel *Kindred*, in which feelings of illness and waves of nausea periodically transport a modern black woman back to the antebellum South, where she lives a parallel, episodic life as a slave. It's a powerful story, too, but it ain't scientific—and that's my concern here.

Equally old hat, now, is to implement time travel simply by having your characters wandering into odd, unfamiliar places. At one time this was a popular device. One of the best of its kind is R.W. Chambers's "The Demoiselle d'Y," which is about a young man who, after getting lost on the coastal moors of France, meets and falls in love with a young lady three centuries in the past. This was interesting when it was published *over a hundred years ago*, and you can find it in the 1895 collection *The King in Yellow* (it's long out of print, so if you want to read it try the interlibrary-loan service described in the bibliography). But don't use this gimmick today, for science fiction. For fantasy, OK, but not for science fiction.

Another once popular method for time traveling was mesmerism. This was used, for example, by University of North Dakota professor John Macnie in his 1883 novel *The Diothas*. In this work (reprinted in 1890 as *A Far Look Forward*) the hero visits the ninety-sixth century (and later returns to his own time by simply falling over a waterfall). It's pretty poor reading today, but at the end there are a few brief, tantalizing words on the ideas of a time traveler being his own ancestor, the possibility of reading an old newspaper while in the future and learning details of life as it will be after returning to the past, and an infinity of parallel worlds. All are puzzles that later would (and still do) fascinate physicists, philosophers and lovers of science fiction. These are good ideas for you to explore, too, and we will in this book. But forget the mesmerism.

Let me mention now that the time travel machines of the past are not the space-time machines of interest to modern science fiction writers (but perhaps may still be of interest for writers of fantasy). Edgar Allen Poe's 1841 "Three Sundays in a Week" achieves its title's remarkable feat simply by crossing time zones in an unusual way and, as it stands, isn't science fiction at all. But the idea was given a real time machine twist in H.S. MacKaye's 1904 novel *The Panchronicon*. A literary time machine with style, the panchronicon (literally a machine "for all times") swings on a rope tether around a huge steel post erected at the North Pole. By "cutting the meridians" faster than the sun does, it travels through space and time from 1898 New Hampshire to the London of three centuries earlier. MacKaye's novel specifically addresses such time-travel paradoxes as changing the past, meeting yourself and causal loops (about which much more will be said in chapter eight). These are ideas that had not been presented before, not even in Wells's *The Time Machine*. *The Panchronicon* also specifically rejects the assertion, often made in early pulp science fiction, that a backwards moving time traveler grows younger. Make this error today, and you'll automatically mark yourself as a scientific illiterate and send your story straight to the reject pile.

Just five years before MacKaye's novel, in 1899, what *seemed* to be a nonfictional essay appeared in the literary journal *Mercure de France*. Authored by the notorious French novelist, poet and artist Alfred Jarry, it seemed to be a description of a real time machine. This was a concept that was all the rage among the literati at that time, of course, because *The Time Machine* had been published just four years earlier. Jarry described his time machine by making an unusual analogy with a gyroscope. Jarry's essay was brought to the attention of the well-known British physicist William Crookes, who then wrote to Oliver Lodge about it. (I gratefully thank the Society for Psychical Research in London, to which both Crookes and Lodge belonged, for providing me with a photocopy of this letter, dated July 7, 1899). Crookes seems to have thought Jarry was serious about how to build a gyroscopic time machine, even though he signed his essay "Doctor Faustroll," which I think a dead giveaway to the true poetic intent of the essay. The gyroscopic time machine analogy is repeated decades later in A.B. Chandler's story "Kelly Country" (which you can find in the anthology *Australian Science Fiction*). Doctor Siebert in that tale explains his time machine: "Imagine a spinning gyroscope. You press down on one end of the axis and it resists the downward pressure. But it does move. It precesses, swings to one side at right angles to the applied force, in the direction of rotation. . . . The rotors of my machine precess, but not through any of the dimensions of normal space. But they precess, nevertheless, within the Space-Time continuum. . . . Temporal precession." The idea is mentioned in passing, too, in A.B. Chandler's story "Castaway," which I'll return to when we get to time travelers meeting themselves in a time loop (you can find that spooky little tale in *Science Fiction Adventures in Dimensions*).

Another machine for a sort of mind travel (which doesn't require a host mind in the past, with only the consciousness of the time traveler actually "traveling") was used in a creepy tale by A.J. Burks,

"When the Graves Were Opened." It was first published in a 1925 issue of the non-science fiction pulp *Weird Tales*—the title speaks for itself. (This pulp, which specialized in fantastic supernatural and horror fiction, was the original publisher of the above-mentioned "Castaway" in 1947.) This is the horrifying story of a time traveler who watches the Crucifixion and the events that follow (from which comes the title—see Matthew 27:52). The author, however, never explains how the process of *watching* is accomplished if the time traveler has no body (and hence no eyes). This is still a good *weird tale*, mind you (it certainly made my skin crawl), but it isn't time-travel science fiction.

So, that's a brief rundown on the sorts of ideas we *won't* be interested in pursuing in this book.

THE PULPS AND TIME TRAVEL

It is in Hugo Gernsback's *Amazing Stories* (starting in April 1926) that we find the first nonfictional speculations about time travel by machine in a pulp magazine. Gernsback started these speculations by reprinting Wells's *The Time Machine*, which sparked a fair number of reader letters that were published in the magazine's "Discussions" section. (Wells's brilliant novella, never out of print since its publication in 1895, will be a central touchstone throughout this book. In 1900, Henry James wrote to Wells simply to express his admiration for Wells's "masterpiece," and to declare to Wells himself "You are very magnificent." High praise, indeed, and praise richly deserved.) Typical of the letters is this excerpt from the July 1927 issue: "In *The Time Machine* I found something amiss. How could one travel to the future in a machine when the beings of the future have not yet materialized?" (The next chapter in this book will give you an answer to that reader's question.) More interesting is the letter from the reader who wrote in that same issue:

> How about this "Time Machine"? Let's suppose our inventor starts a "Time voyage" backward to about A.D. 1900, at which time he was a schoolboy . . . his watch ticks forward

although the clock on the laboratory wall goes backward. Now we are in June 1900, and he stops the machine, gets out and attends the graduating exercises of the class of 1900 of which he was a member. Will there be another "he" on the stage? Of course, because he *did* graduate in 1900. . . . Should he go up and shake hands with this "alter ego"? Will there be two physically distinct but characteristically identical persons? Alas! No! He can't go up and shake hands with himself because . . . this voyage back through time only duplicates actual past conditions and in 1900 this strange "other he" did *not* appear suddenly in quaint ultra-new fashions and congratulate the graduate. How could they both be wearing the same watch they got from Aunt Lucy on their seventh birthday, the same watch in two different places at the same time. Boy! Page Einstein! No, he cannot be there because he wasn't there in 1900 (except in the person of the graduate). . . . The journey backward must cease on the year of his birth. If he could pass *that* year it would certainly be an effect going before a cause. . . . Suppose for instance in the graduating exercise above, the inventor should decide to shoot his former self . . . he couldn't do it because if he did the inventor would have been cut off before he began to invent and he would never have gotten around to making the voyage, thus rendering it impossible for him to be there taking a shot at himself, so that as a matter of fact he *would* be there and *could* take a shot at himself—help, help, I'm on a vicious merry-go-round. . . . Now as to trips into the future, I could probably think up some humorous adventures wherein [the inventor] digs up his own skeleton and finds by the process of actual examination that he must expect to have his leg amputated because the skeleton presents positive proof that this was done.

All of the ingenious puzzles in this letter, enigmatically signed only with the initials T.J.D., intrigued Gernsback (I have always thought that the last lines quoted were the inspiration for R.

Rocklynne's astonishing story "Time Wants a Skeleton," *Astounding Science Fiction*, June 1941), and I doubt it was a coincidence that the same issue featured a new, original time machine story (C.B. White's "The Lost Continent"). This is the tale of a scientist who transports an entire ship at sea 14,000 years back in time and causes it to hover over lost Atlantis. This story provoked a sharp letter from a reader who claimed its logic had a fatal flaw—the story's author indicated the Atlantians observed the time travelers, when "of course" (asserted the reader) the time travelers must actually have been invisible. The reader explained his reasoning as follows, beginning by defining "A" as one of the Atlantians: "Now A lived his life, thousands of years ago, and died. All right, now let us pass on in time 14,000 years. Now, back we come in time when A is again living his life. Lo and behold, this time A sees before he dies a strange phenomenon in the sky! He sees the shipload of people observing him. And yet these people are necessarily observing him during his one and only lifetime, wherein he certainly did not, could not, have observed them." Gernsback printed this letter in his September 1927 editorial "The Mystery of Time" and concluded by saying, "I do . . . agree . . . that the inhabitants of Atlantis would probably not have seen the . . . travelers in time."

Other readers felt the same way, because after Gernsback published yet another time machine story (F. Flagg's "The Machine Man of Ardathia," *Amazing Stories*, November 1927), the same "time travelers must be invisible" argument appeared in the "Discussions" column. Two years later, an amateurishly written tale appeared in which a man travels in time from 1928 to 2930 with the aid of an "astounding machine based on advanced electro-physics and the non-Euclidean theory of hyperspace" (C. Cloukey's "Paradox," *Amazing Stories Quarterly*, Summer 1929). The purpose of this story was twofold: to present several of the classic paradoxes of time travel, and then to make the claim that while the simple minds of twentieth-century people cannot understand the explanations of these paradoxes (perhaps explaining why the author offered none), the paradoxes are all trivial to the scientists of the thirtieth century.

The author, who was ignorant of how to plot a story as well as incapable of writing realistic dialogue, still managed to vastly entertain the readers of the magazine with the sheer mystery of the paradoxes. This story mentions, for example, not only the grandfather paradox but also the much more mysterious causal loop of a time traveler from the future who visits himself in the past to instruct his younger version in building the time machine that will let him visit himself in the past. Letters poured in to the magazine from thrilled young fans, demanding more time travel fiction.

Gernsback was happy to comply. In the December 1929 issue of *Science Wonder Stories* he published H.F. Kirkham's story "The Time Oscillator." (By this time Gernsback had lost control of *Amazing Stories*, and *Science Wonder* was part of his comeback as a publisher of pulp "scientifiction," to use his awful term for science fiction.) This story plays with the questionable role of time travelers in the past—could they actually participate in events ("mix into the affairs of the period," in Gernsback's words) or would they simply be unseen observers? This question, obviously inspired by the earlier discussion in *Amazing Stories*, intrigued Gernsback as much as it did his readers, and along with Kirkham's story he printed a challenge entitled "The Question of Time-Traveling":

> In presenting this story to our readers, we do so with an idea of bringing on a discussion as to time traveling in general. The question in brief is as follows: Can a time traveler, going back in time—whether ten years or ten million years—partake in the life of that time and mingle in with its people, or must he remain suspended in his own time-dimension, a spectator who merely looks on but is powerless to do more? Interesting problems would seem to arise, of which only one need be mentioned: Suppose I can travel back into time, let me say 200 years, and I visit the homestead of my great-grandfather, and am able to take part in the life of his time. I am thus enabled to shoot him, while he is still a young man and as yet unmarried. From this it will be noted that I could have prevented

my own birth, because the line of propagation would have ceased right there. Consequently, it would seem that the idea of time traveling into a past where the time traveler can freely participate in activities of a former age becomes an absurdity. The editor wishes to receive letters from our readers on this point; the best of which will be published in a special section.

Gernsback's challenge did not pass unnoticed, and over the next year or so he published a large number of reader responses in the magazine's letter's column "The Reader Speaks." Indeed, a few months later in his introduction to another story (F. Flagg's "An Adventure in Time," *Science Wonder Stories*, April 1930), Gernsback wrote that ever since the publication of Kirkham's tale "there has been a great controversy among our readers as to the possibility of time flying and the conditions under which it may be done." Most of those letters, and the ones that followed, are interesting but not particularly profound—with one exception. Appearing in the February 1931 issue, this letter (written by San Francisco high school student Jim Nicholson) may well have served as inspiration for several of the classic time-travel tales published during the next twenty years:

> Some time ago you asked us (the readers) what our opinions on time traveling were. Although a bit late, I am now going to voice four opinions . . .

> (1) Now, in the first place, if time traveling were a possibility there would be no need for some scientist getting a headache trying to invent an instrument or "Time-Machine" to "go back and kill grandpa" (in answer to the age-old argument of preventing your birth by killing your grandparents I would say: "who the heck would want to kill his grandpa or grandma!") I figure it out thusly: A man takes a time machine and travels into the future from where he sends it (under automatic control) to the past so that he may find it and travel into the future and send it back to himself again. Hence, the time machine

was never invented, but! . . . from whence did the time machine come?

(2) Another impossibility that might result could be: A man travels a few years into the future and sees himself killed in some unpleasant manner, so, after returning to his correct time he commits suicide in order to avert death in the more terrible way he was destined to. Therefore how could he have seen himself killed in an entirely different manner than really was the case?

(3) Another thing that might corrupt the laws of nature would be to: Travel into the future; find out how some ingenious invention of time worked; return to your right time; build a machine, or whatever it may be, similar to the one you had recently learned the workings of; and use it until the time that saw it arrives, then if your past self saw it as you did, he would take it and claim it to be an invention of his (your) own, as you did. Then—who really *did* invent the consarn thing?

(4) Here's the last knock on time traveling: What if a man were to travel back a few years and marry his mother thereby resulting in his being his own "father"?

[Remember the original 1985 movie *Back to the Future*, with its hint of impending time-travel incest?]

Gernsback's reply to this amazing letter was favorable, opening with "Young Mr. Nicholson does present some of the more humorous[?] aspects of time traveling. Logically we are compelled to admit that he is right—that if people could go back into the past or into the future and partake of the life of those periods, they could disturb the normal course of events."

Nicholson's letter *is* ingenious, and it described the central ideas of many then yet to be written time-travel tales. For example: His Item Two is a precise plot outline of L. Raphael's "The Man Who Saw Through Time" (*Fantastic Adventures*, September 1941); Item Three can be found in Robert Heinlein's *The Door Into Summer*; and a version of Item Four is used in Heinlein's famous short story

"All You Zombies————." Still, as the rest of this book will show, contrary to Gernsback's view, while Nicholson's comments are clever they are not logical.

THE SPECIAL FASCINATION OF TIME-TRAVEL STORIES

Time travel is a literary device that suits many different agendas, a fact that goes a long way, I think, in explaining both the popularity and longevity of this subgenre of science fiction. Travel into the future is an obvious ploy, for example, for writers interested in prophecy. We can find this, in fact, long before the pulps, e.g., in 1856 an anonymously written essay called "January First, A.D. 3000" appeared in *Harper's*. Jules Verne tried his hand at it, too, with "In the Year 2889," written about life a thousand years hence. Neither of these two early efforts involved time travel, but the pulps quickly filled that void, with H. Donitz's "A Visitor From the Twentieth Century" (*Amazing Stories*, May 1928). In this tale, we read of an architect who falls asleep after working hard all day designing a "new" York City for a contest. When he wakes up he is in the last days of the twenty-first century and receives (along with readers) a tour of the far future. Technology has advanced so fast, he is told, that to fly from San Francisco to New York takes "only" ten hours! (When this story was published, of course, it took *days* to fly across the United States—a lesson in failed imagination for all who think they can predict even ten, much less a hundred, years into the future.) We learn at the end that it had all been a dream (another really awful idea for you to avoid in your own stories).

Other stories, too, have used time travel to the future as a literary device to warn against what the end of the world might be like. For example in Philip K. Dick's "Breakfast at Twilight," a family (and their entire house) is suddenly transported seven years into the future, into the middle of a two-year-old atomic war in a world that is a horror of destruction and death. They are told a robot missile attack triggered the transposition of time: "The concentrated energy must have tipped some unstable time fault . . . a *time quake*. . . .

The release of energy . . . sucked your house into the future." A second missile attack later sends them back to their correct time, and the neighbors think the now-ruined house is the result of a faulty water heater explosion. The father doesn't try to explain what really happened—he knows the skeptical reaction he'd get to his tale. The story closes with his understanding of what the future holds: "And when [the war] really came, when the five years were up, there'd be no escape. No going back, tipping back into the past, away from it. When it came for them all, it would have them for eternity."

Reversing direction, time travel to the past is rich with the possibilities of ethical and moral conflict. For example, should a time traveler who gets into a fight in the past with a younger version of *himself* be charged with assault? Could a time traveler who kills in his own time and then escapes into the past be charged with a murder that hasn't yet been committed? If a time traveler abandons a wife in the present and takes another in the past, is he a bigamist? Related issues were the basis for four years of TV's *Quantum Leap*, with the fundamental conflict in each show arising from the ethics of tampering with the past (assuming, for the moment, that this is even possible). And in the 1994 film *Timecop*, we watch a member of the "time police" (charged with the mission of thwarting all who would alter the past for personal gain) tempted by the possibility of preventing the murder of his own wife ten years earlier.

Most obvious of all uses of time travel to the past, of course, is an appeal to nostalgia. This can easily degenerate into the banality of a tearjerker, but if done right (as in Jack Finney's short stories) it can be quite effective.

Time machines and hunting have long had a close association, because stories involving both topics combine time travel with that other wonderful mystery, the *dinosaurs*. For those who like nothing left to the imagination (no gore left unspilled, so to speak), the bloody dinosaur hunts described in David Drake's "Time Safari" and "Boundary Layer" are quite graphic (both are in his 1993 collection *Tyrannosaur*). Far more cerebral is L. Sprague de Camp's 1993 short story collection *Rivers of Time*. Starting with the original 1956 tale, the classic "A Gun for Dinosaur" (which I'll return to later for its description of time-travel paradoxes), these stories continue the adventures of Reginald Rivers, his partner the Raja, and their time-safari-for-hire dinosaur hunts.

OK, you say, so time travel is neat. Who would deny that? But the big question still on your mind, I know, is the one raised both in the Introduction and the beginning of this chapter. Is it, could it really be, *possible*? To be honest, I don't know. But I do know that it is also not known if time travel is impossible. The apparent paradoxes of time travel seem powerful arguments against it, but I like the exchange in Poul Anderson's 1990 novel *The Shield of Time*, a continuation of his time patrol stories. When an operative of the time patrol reveals his identity to a woman of the late twentieth century, she asks, "How does time travel work, anyway? Impossible and absurd, I've read." He replies "According to today's physics and logic, that's true. They'll learn better in the future."

Well, the future is coming faster than even Anderson probably realized, and it is *not* true that today's physics and logic categorically reject time travel. The situation today reminds me of the wonderful exchange between two Edwardian professorial pepperpots, Sumerlee and Challenger, in Sir Arthur Conan Doyle's 1912 novel *The Lost World*. As the two scholars canoe into the uncharted depths of South America, listening to the war drums of unseen, murderous savages, they debate the precise genetic background of their potential enemies. Sumerlee, like Challenger, is of the persuasion that they are cannibals, but adds that they will be "Mongolian in type." Challenger disagrees with this, causing Sumerlee to reply, "I should have thought that even a limited knowledge . . . would have helped to verify it." This provokes a snarl from Challenger (described as a "primitive caveman in a lounge suit"): "No doubt, sir, a limited knowledge would have that effect. When one's knowledge is exhaustive, one comes to other conclusions."

As to whether the time travel debunkers are in possession of limited or exhaustive knowledge, well, we shall see. In his critic's introduction to Robert Heinlein's wonderful time-travel story "All You Zombies————" (in *The Mirror of Infinity*), Alexei Panshin wrote, "Time travel is a philosophical concept, not a scientific one. It is, in fact, as has been pointed out, scientific nonsense." Those words were published in 1970, and there have been a lot of exciting developments in physics since then. I think Panshin would, today, almost certainly want to reconsider his old position, and by the end of this book you'll have your own conclusions.

To be honest, I must admit that Panshin is not the odd-duck-out with his skeptical reaction to time travel. There are many physicists (and yes, science fiction writers, too) who would still agree with his words. But Polish science fiction writer Stanislaw Lem takes a more reasonable position on time travel in a passage from his story "The Twentieth Voyage of Ijon Tichy." He directs his scorn not at time travel itself, but at how some writers have trivialized the subject: "There have been mountains of nonsense written about traveling in time, just as previously there were about astronautics—you know, how some scientist, with the backing of a wealthy businessman, goes off in a corner and slaps together a rocket, which the two of them—and in the company of their lady friends, yet—then take to the far end of the Galaxy. Chronomotion, no less than Astronautics, is a colossal enterprise, requiring tremendous investments, expenditures, planning. . . ."

An amusing story Lem might have had in mind is Sam Mines's "Find the Sculptor" (*Thrilling Wonder Stories*, Spring 1946). In the story, we find the lab assistant to the inventor of the first time machine putting the finishing touches on the gadget with the words: "There it is. The first blasted time machine. Put together by the ingenuity of man and a lot of old kitchen stoves, auto bodies and retired frying pans." Is it any wonder that Lem readily dismissed such stories that reduce space (and time) travel to weekend adventures in a home workshop-laboratory? Don't repeat this awful blunder (unless you are *trying* to be funny).

As I said before, I don't know if time travel is possible or not. However, if time travel is possible, I am fairly sure it won't be easy.

It is likely that there will be some tough times ahead for would-be time machine inventors. It will surely be a challenge even for a genius like Arthur Levitt (the inventor of mind transference through time in A. Weiner's "One More Time"), who was so brilliant "he had built a working computer mainly from string and old TV sets at the age of eleven." Indeed, in Frank Belknap Long's tale "A Guest in the House," it takes a child genius with an IQ of 270 just to fix the broken time machine found abandoned in a cellar.

Before we see a working time machine, I am certain there will be many episodes like the one described in the very funny, 1993 novel-length spoof of academic research *Dr. Dimension* by John DeChancie and David Bischoff. Anyone who has tried to get a stubborn piece of apparatus to work, apparatus that should work and yet simply won't (like a snowblower during a storm), will appreciate Professor Demetrios Demopoulos' frustration and will, I'm sure, forgive him for his intemperate language:

> [T]he distinguished physicist took a step back and, arms akimbo, surveyed the complex and sophisticated machine that was the culmination of years of dedicated scientific research and painstaking technological development.
>
> "What a pile of s---," he said.
>
> "Oh, no, Dr. Demopoulos, don't say that!"
>
> "Well, it is." A sneer formed on the professor's thin lips. "Time machine, my ass. This thing couldn't give you the time, much less travel in it."
>
> "But we haven't incorporated all our latest test data yet," the pretty research assistant reminded him. "These last few adjustments might do it, Professor."
>
> "Hell, we've been tinkering with it for two years," Demetrios complained. "We've tried everything and it's all come to dog poop."

This chapter opened with a discussion of the pulps, and of skepticism toward time travel. Let me close it on the same topics, by quoting from a non-fictional essay by the well-known science fiction writer Harry Harrison ("With a Piece of Twisted Wire . . . ," *SF Horizons*, 1965). He writes, "I used to moan over the fact that pulp magazines were printed on pulp paper and steadily decompose back towards the primordial from which they sprang. I am beginning to feel that this is a bit of a good thing." I believe this statement reflects Harrison's opinion of the pulps' generally shoddy treatment of real science: "[Science fiction] cannot be good without respect for good science." Keep this in mind when you write your time-travel stories.

SUMMARY

This chapter discussed both the initial skeptical reaction most people have to the idea of time travel, and the important distinction between science and fantasy treatments of time travel. Despite their skepticism, most people find time travel irresistible because of the fantasy aspect, and the early pulp magazines were quick to respond to the demand of a growing audience for such imaginative stories. Many of the first sophisticated discussions of the time travel paradoxes took place in the tales and letters columns of the pulps, and later stories showed ever-increasing awareness of the real intellectual puzzles of time travel.

CHAPTER 2

Special Relativity and Time Travel to the Future

[The] equations of duo-quadrant lineations [have] been substantiated. . . . Our fourth-angle deviation from the six conceivable electronic dimensions did the trick all right. I went forward in Time.

a 1930s science fiction scientist babbles incoherent nonsense, not science, in a pulp magazine story about how to travel into the future in J.H. Haggard's "He Who Masters Time" (*Thrilling Wonder Stories*: February 1937).

Time is a mysterious concept, a mystery that becomes ever more unclear the older one gets. It has always been so. The ancients were as perplexed by the nature of time as we are today. We learn from Plutarch's *Platonic Questions* that, when questioned about time's nature, Pythagoras could only utter the mystical "time is the soul of this world." Centuries later, Saint Augustine wrote in his *Confessions*,

"What, then, is time? I know well enough what it is, provided that nobody asks me; but if I am asked what it is and try to explain, I am baffled." And many centuries after that, the French philosopher Henri Bergson did his best (in his 1888 doctoral dissertation) by declaring that time is "nothing but the ghost of space haunting the reflective consciousness." Well, maybe, but time is still a mystery to me.

Despite the mystery, I think most people would agree that we can at least divide time into the three categories of *past*, *present* and *future*. But even that may be too hasty an agreement. One early pulp science fiction writer, for example, had some fun with this supposed division of time in a story that reads like many of today's scholarly philosophical journals (L.A. Eshbach, "The Time Conqueror," *Wonder Stories*, July 1932). This tale contains a long discussion between a mad scientist and his victim (whose brain, in time-honored pulp magazine tradition, winds up in a vat) on the nature of time. At one point, the mad scientist delivers an interesting lecture on the "present." After he gets his victim to declare that the past no longer exists and the future does not yet exist, the mad scientist argues that such a position means "the present is the moment of transition of a phenomenon from one non-existence to another non-existence—since you say the future and past do not exist. But that short moment we term the present is after all fictional in character; it cannot be measured. We can never seize it. That which we did seize is always the past. So, according to your own conception of time . . . neither past, present nor future exists!"

That argument is immediately rejected by the victim, who exclaims, "But that is absurd! You and I exist, and the world exists—and all in the present." To which the mad scientist responds, "Of course. And that proves the falsity of the popular conceptions of the divisions of time."

Is time (whatever it may be) smoothly continuous? To our crude human senses it appears to be; but if it is not, is there a shortest time? Is there a *time quantum*, a shortest possible time duration that is greater than zero? Quantum mechanics has made the idea of quantized energy a familiar one, and it now appears that quantum mechanics may also impose a similar constraint on time.

As with energy, time may "pass" only in discrete jumps, and "being in-between" two adjacent time values may have no physical meaning. (By our everyday observations of how the world actually works, the difference between two adjacent time jumps would have to be pretty small.) This issue is at the middle of present-day debates on quantum gravity (the union of relativity theory and quantum mechanics), which almost certainly has a strong connection to the possibility that time machines might one day exist.

Much of the present controversy over the possibility of time machines hinges on the *quantum gravity cutoff*. This is a cutoff at some finite value of destructive space-time stresses that otherwise tend to grow toward infinity whenever a time machine attempts to form. The "cutoff" of those stresses supposedly occurs in instances when the terminal phase of the stress blow-up takes place in less time than the minimum possible interval (and, of course, nothing can actually be less than the minimum). The debate is over just what the minimum duration is, and if the cutoff would occur before the stresses could reach sufficiently high *finite* values as to exceed the material strength of any possible structure and so destroy the time machine anyway. I discuss this cutoff in greater depth in chapter eleven.

The modern time-travel debate concerns travel into the *past*. As you will soon see, time travel to the future is not in question among physicists, not even those (like Stephen Hawking) who believe travel to the past would lay waste to physics as we know it. As S. Deser and R. Jakiw (two other physicist-critics of time travel to the past) have written, "After 1900, special relativity made scientific discussion of time machines possible."

EINSTEIN'S DISCOVERY OF THE RELATIVITY OF TIME

One of the predictions of the special theory of relativity (which actually dates from 1905) is that moving clocks run slow compared to stationary clocks, a result called *time dilation*. This conclusion was a stupendous shock to the scientists of the day, Victorian scientists trained in the tradition of Newton. It was Newton himself who declared in 1687 (in the *Scholium* to the *Definitions* of his masterpiece *Principia*), "Absolute true and mathematical time, of itself, and from its own nature, flows equally without relation to anything external, and by another name is called *duration*." Einstein said, in effect, that Newton had made a mistake.

So, how did Einstein arrive at his amazing conclusion about time which has figured in so many time-travel stories? First, let me give you a little history (and jargon, that you can use in your fiction). Our discussion in this chapter will incorporate a lot of math, but don't allow that to daunt you. The equations are presented here as *reference* points. The general concepts behind the math will be explored in depth for use in your stories.

Imagine two three-dimensional coordinate systems (what physicists call "frames of reference"), one of which we'll take to be stationary and the other as moving with respect to the first. Let this motion be a constant speed denoted by the symbol v. We can orient these two coordinate systems so that the motion of the moving one occurs along (is coincident with) just one axis—let's call it the x-axis. The other two dimensions (denoted by y and z) are also always parallel with their analogous dimensions in the moving frame. I'll use primed variables to denote the moving frame (see Figure 2.1).

Suppose also that there is a clock at the origin of each frame, and that at the instant the two origins coincide in space we synchronize the clocks; i.e., when the origins match we have $t = t' = 0$. Finally, imagine there are two observers (as physicists say), one sitting on the origin in each frame. These two observers have agreed that at some arbitrary instant of time, each will record the coordinates of some (arbitrary, previously agreed upon) point in space, as measured in his frame. For example, there could be a red balloon floating in space whose location will be recorded when the observers' respective clocks read $t = 5$ seconds. It seems immediately obvious (as it did for Newton) that $t = t'$ all the time, i.e., time runs at the same rate in each frame, and it therefore makes sense to talk about the "same instant" for each observer.

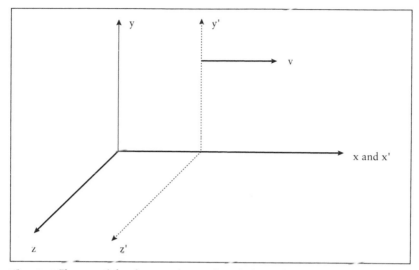

Fig. 2-1 Two spatial reference frames in relative motion.

So, at the "same instant," the stationary observer records the three space coordinates of the balloon (x, y, z) in his frame, and the moving observer records the three space coordinates of the balloon (x', y', z') in *his* frame. A physicist now asks, what are the relationships between the primed and unprimed coordinates; that is, what mathematical transformation converts from one frame of reference to the other? The answer seems obvious: Since the relative motion is along the x direction only, the y and z coordinates are unchanged, and the x coordinate changes linearly with both time and speed. Thus:

$$y' = y$$
$$z' = z$$
$$x' = x - vt.$$

This transformation, called the *Galilean transformation* after the Italian Galileo Galilei (1564–1642), satisfies the principle which says uniform motion leaves the laws of physics unchanged. That is, the stationary observer and the uniformly moving observer would arrive at the same laws of physics (e.g., the conservation laws of energy and momentum, Newton's laws, Kepler's laws, etc.). More precisely, the laws of *mechanics* (which describe how matter will move in response to applied forces) are the same for both observers. Any frame of reference in which Newton's laws of mechanics hold true is said to be *inertial*. Given one inertial frame, we can find another simply by applying the Galilean transformation.

However, when Scotsman James Clerk Maxwell (1832–1879) discovered the mathematical laws of electrodynamics (which describe how electric and magnetic fields are related to each other and to electrical change in matter), the Galilean transformation did not leave Maxwell's equations unchanged; i.e., the transformation equations above predict electromagnetic effects in the moving system that are not predicted to occur in the stationary system (ether, an all-pervading substance, was supposed to be the stationary system, the "something" through which electromagnetic waves, like light, could travel). This means that there was theoretical support for the possibility that electromagnetic experiments might be devised to detect uniform motion, and this eventually led to the famous Nobel Prize-winning Michelson-Morley experiment of 1887. This experiment, sensitive enough to detect the motion (if any) of the Earth relative to the supposed ether, failed to detect any such motion. The conclusion was clear—the extra electromagnetic effects predicted by the Galilean transformation simply did not exist, so the transformation must not work with electromagnetics, even though it works with the laws of mechanics. What is the explanation?

The answer is inspired, and again returns to the very cornerstone of relativity: The laws of physics, *all* the laws of physics, should look the same to observers in uniform relative motion. By the end of the nineteenth century, evidence from a very broad variety of experiments had convinced people that Maxwell's equations were correct. If Maxwell's theory were wrong, for example, then radios wouldn't work. Thus, the discovery of a new transformation, which would leave both the laws of mechanics and the laws of electrodynamics unchanged by uniform motion, was necessary. A single transformation that would work on Maxwell's equations *and* on the mechanical laws would mean that Newton's mechanical laws could not be correct. This conclusion was breathtaking, as Newton had been unchallenged for two centuries.

However, it turns out that Newton's laws are almost right. The following concept is the only correction required: The mass, m, of a moving body is not independent of speed, but rather varies as

$$m = \frac{m_0}{\sqrt{1-(v/c)^2}},$$

where m_0 is the *rest mass* (the mass when $v=0$) and c denotes the speed of light (186,200 miles per second, or thereabouts). Don't worry about why the mass varies like this; it is not intuitive. It's just the way the world works.

Pay particular attention to the square root in the denominator. It turns up, over and over, all through relativity theory. It turns up so much let's agree to give it a special name—the "Lorentz factor," which I'll write as *LF*. Notice, in particular, that *LF* is equal to 1 when $v=0$, and to 0 when $v=c$. *LF* is *imaginary* (the square root of a negative number) when v is greater than c, and this is one reason for the often heard statement "nothing can move faster than light." That is, v is usually less than c, and only light itself travels at the speed of light. This will be important to remember when we get to faster-than-light (FTL) physics and how it connects to time travel.

The variation of mass with speed was experimentally observed in 1901 by the German Walter Kaufmann (1871–1947) before Einstein published the special theory. This strange effect shows that m is infinite at $v=c$ (unless $m_0=0$, as it is for a particle of light, the photon) because the Lorentz factor is zero. (Zero divided by zero is undefined, mathematically meaningless and *not* infinite.) This calculation supports the assertion that accelerating a nonzero mass (i.e., a spaceship) to the speed of light is impossible because it would require infinite energy (due to the spaceship's infinite mass at the speed of light). With this single modification, the transformation equations that leave *all* the laws of physics unaltered by uniform motion are:

$$y' = y$$
$$z' = z$$
$$x' = (x - vt)/LF$$
$$t' = [t - (vx/c^2)]/LF.$$

These equations are called the *Lorentz transformation*, after the Dutchman Hendrik Antoon Lorentz (1853–1928) who discovered them in 1904 by a direct mathematical manipulation of Maxwell's equations. It was Einstein, however, who in 1905 showed how to derive the transformation equations from a fundamental reexamination of space and time, without concern for the details of specific laws. Notice, in particular, how the transformation equations that relate t and t', and x and x', have both variables in them. That is, the time transformation involves space, and the space transformation involves time. This is mathematical physics weaving space and time together into a single entity that has come to be called *space-time* (a concept actually due not to Einstein, but to his college math teacher Hermann Minkowski—more on him in the next chapter).

The folding together of space and time is of fundamental interest to science fiction writers because the modern scientific theory of time travel is Einstein's theory of *curved space-time* (the distinction between curved and flat space-time is somewhat analogous to the distinction between the curved roof of a football stadium and the flat surface of the stadium's parking lot). The theory of flat space-time is better known as the *special* theory of relativity, while the theory of curved space-time is the *general* theory of relativity.

Early science fiction writers were aware of this mixing of space and time by relativity, but sometimes they didn't really know what it meant. Consider, for example, how one writer mangled the concept (V. Rousseau, "The Atom Smasher," *Astounding Stories*, May 1930): As an evil scientist is using a time machine to transport captives into the past, he tells them, "We've got a longish journey before us, ten thousand years more, multiplied by the fourth power of two thousand miles." That sort of stuff could dazzle the teenagers of 1930, but it'll just get you hoots of laughter today (ask yourself what the dimensional units of that odd little calculation are). You could say, with equal (non)sense, that the length of a space-time journey is "an apple plus a pear, divided by the cube root of a banana."

There are many strange implications tucked away in the Lorentz transformation equations, all quite contrary to our everyday intuitions. That is because our intuitions have developed in a world in which everything around us happens at speeds far less than that of light. At such low speeds the Galilean transformation is an excellent approximation, which explains why Newton's laws of mechanics were accepted for two hundred years without any suspicion that they might not be absolutely correct. For those who are interested, the mathematical details in support of these implications can be found in my book *Time Machines*; I will simply state four of them here.

First, clocks run slow in a moving frame, compared to clocks in a stationary frame. In fact, with just a little high school algebra (which I will not make you slog through) it can be shown that if we look just at $x' = 0$ (which is where the moving clock is located) then the Lorentz equations reduce to $t' = t \times LF$. This says $t' = t$ if $v = 0$ (which makes sense, since if $v = 0$ then the "moving" frame is really not moving), and that $t' = 0$ if $v = c$. This second conclusion *is* really odd, because $t' = 0$ no matter *what* t may be; i.e., when $v = c$ "time stands still." For example, a traveler leaving the surface of a star 100 light years from Earth (the traveler is a photon) would require 100 years to reach Earth, as measured by an Earth-based clock. For the photon, however, the journey requires *zero time*; i.e., the trip is instantaneous, and the photon arrives on Earth the instant after it leaves the star. This would be the case even if the star were on the other side of the universe.

Second, two events that are seen as simultaneous in one inertial frame are not necessarily seen as simultaneous in another inertial frame. As Einstein's friend Kurt Gödel (more on him in chapter seven) wrote, "The very starting point of relativity theory consists in the discovery of a new and very astounding property of time, namely the relativity of simultaneity."

Third, a modification in the length of an extended object, similar

THE LORENTZ TIME-SLOWING EFFECT	
v/c	1/LF
spaceship	Earth
0.1	1.005
0.2	1.021
0.5	1.155
0.7	1.4
0.9	2.294
0.999	22.366
0.9999	70.712

to that of time, occurs with motion. If the length of the object (along the direction of motion) is measured to be L' by an observer moving with the object (and so to her the object appears stationary), then the observer in the stationary frame will measure the length to be $L = L' \times LF$. That is, the object will appear to the stationary observer to be contracted. This effect is called the *Lorentz-FitzGerald contraction*; the Irish physicist George Francis FitzGerald (1851–1901) put the contraction idea forward in 1889 as an ad hoc suggestion, with no theoretical basis, to explain the results of the Michelson-Morley experiment I mentioned earlier.

The time-slowing (or length-contraction) factor becomes pronounced only at values of v close to c; the table above shows this effect. For example, the last entry says that a clock traveling on a rocketship at 99.99 percent the speed of light will register the passage of 1 year while nearly 71 years pass on Earth.

One science fiction writer got this dramatically wrong, even though he actually reproduced the Lorentz factor in his story (L.R. Hubbard, "To the Stars," *Astounding Science Fiction*, February and March 1950). He writes of a near-light-speed rocketship, "If it [the ship's speed] was as slow as ninety-four percent [of the speed of light] . . . for every moment ticked by the clocks of the [ship] hundreds passed on Earth." In fact, the time-dilation factor at that speed is only 2.931.

This isn't quite as bad as the errors that the early pulp writers made. For example, in J.H. Haggard's "Faster Than Light" (*Wonder Stories*, October 1930), the story of a runaway spaceship falling into the Sun, we find: "When our racing [ship] was drawn from the Earth's gravity and fell at ever increasing speed toward the Sun it soon approached the speed of light. As we fell faster and faster our length in the direction of the sun progressed into nothingness. Then—it reached the speed of light—passed it. Now—mind you this—when the ship attained the speed of light it was of a *minus* length." There are three errors here, as a spaceship could never reach the speed of light, could certainly not exceed it, and if it did, its contracted length as observed from Earth would not be negative but imaginary (if such a quantity could be observed). Making such errors today will be instantly fatal to a story.

First prize for mangling relativistic physics has to go to N. Schachner's "Reverse Universe" (*Astounding Stories*, June 1936). In this tale, a spaceship is on its way to Alpha Centauri at near light speed when the crew mutinies and puts the captain and first officer "overboard" in a space boat with six months' provisions. Since this happens mid-voyage, about two light years from both home and destination, matters look grim. The author tells us several times that things look very bad, indeed. But are they necessarily fatal? With a stated speed of 162,000 miles per second, the time-dilation factor is 2.028; since the space boat is traveling at $0.87c$, it will take a little less than fourteen months of space-boat time to complete the journey. (That is, $2/0.87 = 2.299$ years time to travel two light years as measured by an Earth-based clock. It is the space-boat clock, however, that measures the time experienced by the two men, and it measures $2.299/2.028 = 1.13$ years $= 13.6$ months.)

If the two men go on half-rations, then it seems they could survive. There is, of course, the problem of slowing down so as to arrive at Alpha Centauri at a reasonable speed, but Schachner ignored that concern. Indeed, his attention was directed to a much more dramatic conclusion. He had, I kid you not, a faster-than-light planet (please don't ask how that was explained) collide from behind and carry the castaways on toward their destination! While on the FTL planet, time runs backward; but for what *really* happens at super-luminal speeds, see chapter ten.

And finally, for the fourth strange implication of the Lorentz transformation, let me tell you about the addition-of-velocities problem. Suppose you are in a high-speed spaceship traveling away from Earth at speed v. The Earth is our stationary frame, and the spaceship is the moving frame; assume that the x and x' axes are along the direction of motion. Imagine next that you fire a gun inside the spaceship, toward the nose of the spaceship, with the bullet exiting the muzzle at speed w. How fast is the bullet moving away from the Earth? The commonsense Galilean transformation says $v + w$, but now you know that this transformation is wrong. What does the Lorentz transformation say? After doing the math, the answer is

$$(w + v)/[1 + (wv)/c^2.]$$

Notice that for a low-speed bullet (w is much smaller than c) this gives a result that is close to $w + v$ (don't forget that v is less than c, too).

Now, suppose you don't fire a gun, but instead replace the gun with a flashlight. Instead of a bullet, you are "shooting" photons with a speed of $w = c$. The Galilean transformation would say that a stationary observer (with respect to Earth) in front of the spaceship would see the photons flash by at a speed of $v + c$, which is a faster-than-light or *superluminal* speed. The Lorentz transformation, on the other hand, says the stationary observer would see the photons flash by at a speed of

$$(c + v)/[1 + (cv)/c^2] = c^2(c + v)/(c^2 + cv)$$
$$= c^2(c + v)/[c(c + v)] = c.$$

That is, no matter what the speed v of the spaceship, the stationary observer sees the photons traveling at the same speed (c) as does the moving observer. The speed of light is, in fact, the only speed that comes out of the velocity-addition formula the same as it goes in. The speed of light is said to be an invariant, and it is this property of light that physicists consider to be reflective of light's special place in the way things work (not that the speed of light is some sort of "ultimate" speed).

A failure to understand the implications of the special theory resulted in three additional errors in the pulp magazine story of a near-light-speed rocketship ("To the Stars") mentioned before. At all times, an officer stands watch on the bridge of this ship to be sure the ship doesn't accidently reach the speed of light. This is to be avoided (according to the author) because to reach the speed of light would cause the ship to "hang there forever, unmoving [in time] . . . locked, protected and condemned to eternity by zero time." You'll recall from my previous example of the photon traveling to Earth from a star one hundred light years distant that this is not what is meant by saying "time stands still" at the speed of light.

Reaching the speed of light is so easy in this story (according to the author, who was apparently unaware it would require infinite energy) that occasionally the ship has to fire a "checkblast" from its forward rocket tubes to slow down. Equally absurd is the means by which the development of this "irreversible" condition is detected—a forward-pointing light source is mounted on the nose of the ship, and the ship is getting too near the speed of light if it overtakes the photons emitted by the source.

THE PARADOX OF THE TWINS

Special relativity says that by traveling in a rocketship close to the speed of light you could leave Earth, loop out on a vast journey halfway across the universe, and then return hundreds, thousands, even millions of years in the future. You could do this, in fact, with minimal passage of your *proper time* (time as measured by your wristwatch or the beating of your heart). This wonderful use of rocket as time machine to the future was first noted by the French physicist Paul Langevin in 1911. Many years later, it was observed that the same effect could, when used in conjunction with *wormholes* (discussed in chapter nine), be used to build a time machine to travel backwards into the past.

Physicists generally believed, in fact, that *any* kind of motion (not just uniform-speed, straight-line motion) slows time down in precise accordance with the time dilation formula of special relativity. This is called the *clock hypothesis*, and it has been experimentally checked in various special circumstances. For example, in one 1960 experiment, the rate of time kept by atomic clocks (i.e., decaying radioactive atoms) accelerated beyond 66,000 gees precisely matched the time-dilation prediction of special relativity (one gee is the acceleration of Earth's gravity field at the surface of the planet). The accelerations generated in this experiment were produced with a rapidly spinning disk (remember merry-go-rounds and the acceleration forces that had you hanging on with both hands when you were a kid?). One amusing (but dizzy) design for a time machine to the future would be a very souped-up clothes dryer. (This is an idea I have not seen used yet in a story—I give it to you for free.)

With the clock hypothesis as theoretical support, you can now understand the relativistic time puzzle called the *paradox of the twins*. The situation is simple—one of two twins will always remain on Earth, while the other will take a long, high-speed rocketship trip out into space and back. The space-traveling twin is, as it turns out, also a time traveler into the future. Here's how it works.

To begin her journey, the space- (and time-) traveling twin gets into the rocketship at time $t = t' = 0$ (remember, t is time measured on Earth, and t' is time measured on the rocket). The Earth and rocket clocks are synchronized at the instant of departure. Let's assume that the rocket trip is to be made in comfort, so the rocket accelerates at a constant value. (In the numerical values I'll give you in just a bit, this constant acceleration will be one gee, which is equivalent to Earth's surface gravity (an acceleration we all live with through our entire lives), and two gees, to which perhaps most humans could adapt without too much discomfort.

The traveling twin does this for a time interval of T (as measured

EXPERIENCED ACCELERATION = ONE GEE	
$4T'$ (rocket time, in years)	$4T$ (Earth time, in years)
1	1.01
2	2.09
5	6.5
7	11.5
10	25.5
20	339
30	4,478
40	59,223

on Earth) and T' (as measured on the rocket). Then she turns off the rearward engine and turns on a forward mounted engine to experience a constant deceleration. Other than the fact that floor and ceiling interchange, the traveling twin always weighs the same and there is no change in the experienced environment. If she does this for the same time interval as before (T in earth time, T' in rocket time), the rocket will be brought to rest with respect to the now-distant Earth. The traveling twin next simply repeats the process in the reverse direction, first accelerating for T (T') and decelerating for T (T'). The traveling twin thus arrives back home with a final speed of zero with respect to Earth (ignoring, of course, all the navigational problems due to the motion of Earth during the trip).

The total duration of the trip has been $4T$ in Earth time, and $4T'$ in rocket time. The twin paradox is the claim that $4T'$ is less than $4T$, and that in fact it can be a lot less. The mathematical details can, again, be found in my book *Time Machines*, but the table above (and on the next page) show some typical numerical results.

As these two tables show, time dilation would allow humans to literally travel to the stars (in distance) as well as through time into the future. But only at a terrible price. If there is no way to travel backwards in time, then one is trapped in the future. The central character in the story "To the Stars" considers this very predicament

EXPERIENCED ACCELERATION = TWO GEES	
$4T'$ (rocket time, in years)	$4T$ (Earth time, in years)
1	1.04
2	2.4
5	12.7
7	35.9
10	169.9
20	29,612
30	5,180,000
40	906 million(!)

as he is shanghaied by the crew; "And there was a real frenzy in him. . . . He knew all about the Lorentz-Einstein Relativity Equations. He knew what happened when a ship got to ninety-nine percent of the speed of light. . . . As mass approaches the speed of light, time approaches zero. It was his sentence . . . to forever."

The idea of a rocketship pilot (call him Bob) returning to Earth while still young, while all those he left behind (say his twin brother, Bill) have become old (or dead), has entered both physics and fictional literature as the twin paradox. The reason this situation is called a paradox is not because of the time-travel aspect (there are no logical paradoxes with travel only into the future), but because it seems to violate the very spirit of relativity. That is, from Bill's point of view, Bob at first travels away and then returns. But one might argue that from Bob's point of view it is Bill (and the entire Earth) who first recedes and then returns. So why is it *Bob* who is younger? The answer is that the two points of view are actually not identical, and that there is a definite asymmetry between Bill and Bob. After all, it is Bob who feels the acceleration from the rocket's engines, who feels forces, while Bill feels nothing unusual back on Earth.

At the beginning of a very nice, readable discussion of the twin paradox, the physicist A. Schild wrote, "I have no doubt that if our technology should ever advance to the stage where large-scale twin effects become noticeable with our unaided senses, then [people] will have no difficulty in adjusting their concepts of time until the new phenomena seem quite natural." Well, perhaps, but perhaps not. A. Schild had not read D.I. Masson's fascinating story "Traveler's Rest." That tale is based on the bizarre human problems caused by time distortions on a planet where time passes ever more slowly as one moves upward in latitude. No physical explanation is given for this temporal distortion, but relativistic time dilation would be equivalent in effect. In printed fiction, you can't do better than to read Robert Heinlein's 1956 novel *Time for the Stars*.

Some modern philosophers are still not quite sure about traveling into the future. For example, after mentioning time dilation in his 1981 book, *Real Time*, philosopher D. Mellor declared that freezing and sleeping are equally valid ways to travel into the future; he wrote, "Rip van Winkle was a time traveller . . . and so in its humble way is every hibernating animal. All in all, real forward time travel is . . . really only an overly grand description of processes slowing down or stopping." Because he considers sleeping or being frozen equivalent to time dilation, this philosopher calls forward time travel a "trifling topic." The year before, philosopher W. Godfrey-Smith had agreed, declaring "forward time travel may be dismissed as boring." I think this assessment incorrect. Let me now treat these two points, time travel to the future as "trivial" and as "boring," in order.

First, I think the characterization of time travel to the future as "trifling" represents ignorance of the concept of proper time, despite Mellor's passing nod toward special relativity's time dilation. Time dilation is not equivalent to either sleeping or freezing. (But I must admit Hollywood seems fascinated with freezing as a way to get characters into the future—the first half of the 1990s alone had the films *Late for Dinner*, *Encino Man*, *Forever Young*, and *Demolition Man*.) That is, suppose that when you deposit a friend in his deep freezer you compare his wristwatch with yours and find they are synchronized. Years later, when you thaw your friend, you will find the two watches still agree. But if another friend's watch agreed with yours at the moment she was climbing into a rocket ship to begin the space journey I discussed earlier, then upon her return to Earth years later you will find her watch is far behind yours. The passage of time has been the same for you and your frozen friend, but not the same for you and your space traveling friend. Your friend in the rocketship experienced time (travel) dilation, while your friend in the freezer simply slowed his metabolic processes by a direct physical intervention of the aging process that rendered him unconscious.

Your friend in space, however, has consciously lived through her experience, which has seemed perfectly normal to her. There is a marvelous scene in the 1960 film *The Time Machine* that illustrates this phenomenon. When the time traveller first tests his gadget, he attempts to go forward only a brief time; he isn't sure he has been successful until he compares a wall clock in his lab with his own pocket watch.

Not all philosophers have failed to grasp the subtle nuances of proper time. One has, for example, recently given a very pretty description of the psychological implications of proper time. This philosopher, A. Gallois, begins his discussion of the distinction between the proper time of a time traveler and the time of his friends who stay at home by asking what appears to be a question with an obvious answer. Suppose you suddenly wake up in a hospital and are told you have been in a coma for the past two weeks. You are also told that you were in an auto accident two weeks ago, you suffered temporary neural damage and that the eventual reversal of such damage always, at some time within four weeks after the damage occurs, causes a day of excruciating pain if you are conscious at the time. Would you prefer the day of damage reversal to be in the past two weeks (when you were in the coma), or in the next two weeks? The answer seems obvious. After all, if the day that damage reversal occurs has already happened then you simply slept through it and missed the pain. To prefer the day of pain to be in the future (when you presumably will be conscious) seems absurd. You would almost certainly want that day to be in your past. Now, let's add time travel to the equation.

All is as before, but now you immediately leave the hospital to take a time trip back to 1892 where you will stay for two weeks. Again, it seems clear that you would prefer to have had the day of pain in the past two weeks, not in the next two weeks (in 1892). Notice that the *next* is a reference to your proper time; while 1892 is the global past, it is your personal future. So, your preference would be to have the day of pain in the *recent* past, not the *distant* past (globally) of 1892. Now, let's add another time travel twist to this story.

All is as before in the original tale, except now you are told that the auto accident happened just after you made a time trip to 2092; i.e., as you walked out of your time machine in 2092 you were hit by a car. The two weeks you were in the coma were in 2092, before being judged fit enough (although still unconscious) to make the time journey back to this year. When would you now prefer to have the day of pain? Clearly, as always, in your personal past, which is now however the global future. Time for those who time travel *is* different from what it is for those who don't.

Still, while time travel to the future via time dilation may not be either boring or trivial, it is a one-way trip. A trip that is often heart-rending in science fiction. For example, in R.H. Wilson's tale from the 1930's, "Out Around Rigel," a space traveler returns from a high-speed trip to the blue supergiant star Rigel, in the constellation Orion. The 900 or so light-years of the round-trip had required just six months of ship (or proper) time, but a thousand years of Earth time. The traveler returns to find that all he had last seen waving him good-by at the start of his journey are now long dead. He tells of his pain with: "Sometimes I waken from a dream in which they are all so near . . . all my old companions . . . and for a moment I cannot realize how far away they are. Beyond years and years."

Ben Bova's novel *On a Darkling Plain* makes good use of time dilation. It is the story of two lovers parted in time when one makes a decades-long (Earth time) trip to the star Sirius and back.

To avoid such emotional tragedies (and also to get into the fun of paradoxes), science fiction writers need some way to get their characters back from the future, some theory for how to travel back to the past that is actually the "present" for them. With backwards time travel it becomes possible to wonder (and to write stories) about the possibility that someday, for example, scientists might return with color photographs of Mount Vesuvius burying Pompeii in A.D. 79; one evening television viewers might tune in to watch a time traveling historian's videotape of a huge wooden horse being dragged inside the walls of Troy on a fateful day in 1250 B.C. But first, we need that theory. That is the topic of the next chapter.

SUMMARY

In this chapter, you've learned how the well-established *special theory of relativity* provides solid theoretical support for the possibility of time travel into the future with the use of very high speed rocketships. We have discussed the special role in physics played by the speed of light, and why it is believed to be the ultimate speed. The theoretical concepts of *reference frames, frame transformation* (equations), *proper time, time dilation* and the *twin paradox* have also been discussed and illustrated with examples from science fiction (using both good *and* goofy science).

CHAPTER 3

Time Travel to the Past

"You mean that time travel really is possible? That men can be transported into the future or the past—"

The other held up a restraining hand. "Yes. Time travel is possible. . . ."

"But professor! Think what you're saying! You're telling me that I could go back and murder my own grandfather. That I could prevent myself from being born—"

Again the elder sighed. "I was afraid of this," he said. "I knew you could not understand." He hesitated. Then: "At any rate, take my word for it that time travel is possible."

> a young hero and a brilliant old scientist chat in C. South's "The Time Mirror" (*Amazing Stories*: December 1942).

Time travel into the past has to be one of the most popular fantasies. Some years ago the philosopher Jan Faye nicely captured this yearning when he wrote, "We all from time to time indulge in dreams about traveling back into time. Every time we recall something that happened in the past we make a mental journey back in time. But wouldn't it be grand if we could actually return physically to the most delightful moments of our memories? Wouldn't we all like to reexperience the bliss of childhood and the heyday of youth, or return to make that big decision that we failed to make then for lack of courage?" Nice, yes, but is it really possible? Apparently the

nineteenth-century American educator Horace Mann didn't think
so when he wrote, "Lost yesterday, somewhere between sunrise
and sunset, two golden hours, each set with sixty diamond minutes.
No reward is offered, for they are gone forever."

Nearly half a century ago, at *The Magazine of Fantasy and Science
Fiction*, the editors seemingly didn't much like the idea of time traveling either, as their introduction to a routine *time-slip* (i.e., a non-
machine) story in the February 1950 issue opened: "Time travel is
impressive enough when elaborately decked out with oddly constructed machines, theories of temporomagnetic fields and formulas
involving the square root of minus one, but you can read such stories
with a reasonable assurance that your own life is never going to
involve such machines, theories or formulas."

The "formulas involving the square root of minus one," that the
editors were talking about, are of course from the Einstein theories
of relativity. And there is no typo there: I really do mean *theories*,
not just theory. In the last chapter I discussed the special theory,
which offers an explanation for time travel to the future. Einstein's
other theory, the *general theory* (dating from 1916), is the key to
understanding time travel to the past.

Before Einstein, the theory of gravity used by scientists was
Newton's, a theory that, while amazingly accurate under most situations, does have tiny (but still observable) errors in certain astronomical applications. In addition, Newton's theory is a purely de-
scriptive one, allowing the calculation of gravitational effects without
offering any explanation for gravity. Not only does Einstein's general
theory of relativity always give the right answers (even in those
cases where Newton's doesn't), it also explains gravity. It does this
by treating the world as a four-dimensional one in which all four
dimensions (three space and one time) are, in a certain sense, on
equal footing. The resulting geometrical description of the world—
actually due to the German mathematician Hermann Minkowski
(1864–1909), who was one of Einstein's teachers in Zurich, Switzer-
land—is that of a unified space-time, while Newton's theory keeps
space and time separate and distinct.

Since 1905, physicists have known that Einstein's special theory allows time travel to the future. To return, however, to travel backward through time into the past, had been thought to be impossible until 1949. Since then the general theory, which allows time travel to the past under certain special conditions, has passed every experimental test to which it has been subjected. This is not a widely known fact, even among many science fiction writers and other technically trained people. It is the availability of this scientific theory that separates time travel speculations and claims from the fantasy notions with which they are often unjustly lumped (e.g., ESP, astrology and mind-over-matter).

Three years after Einstein published the formal mathematical theory of special relativity, his former math teacher, Minkowski, showed how to interpret Einstein's equations geometrically in four-dimensional hyperspace. (More on hyperspace in the next chapter.) With his "geometrization" of special relativity, Minkowski was to have a profound influence in physics that continues to this day. His famous 1908 paper, "Space and Time," was delivered orally; his words were electrifying then and still are today.

Minkowski began dramatically: "Gentlemen! The views of space and time which I wish to lay before you have sprung from the soil of experimental physics, and therein lies their strength. They are radical." Then comes the famous line (quoted in so many freshman college physics textbooks and philosophy papers) concerning space-time: "Henceforth space by itself, and time by itself, are doomed to fade away into mere shadows, and only a kind of union of the two will preserve independence."

Minkowski explained what space-time is in these enthusiastic words to his audience:

> A point of space at a point of time . . . I will call a *world-point*. The multiplicity of all thinkable *x, y, z, t* systems of values we will christen the *world*. With this most valiant piece of chalk I might project upon the blackboard four world axes . . . Not to leave a yawning void anywhere, we will imagine that

everywhere and everywhen there is something perceptible. To avoid saying "matter" or "electricity" I will use for this something the word "substance." We fix our attention on the substantial point which is at the world-point x, y, z, t; and imagine that we are able to recognize this substantial point at any other time. Let the variations dx, dy and dz of the space coordinates of this substantial point correspond to the time element dt. Then we obtain, as an image, so to speak, of the everlasting career of the substantial point, a curve in the world, a *world-line*. . . . The whole Universe is seen to resolve itself into similar world-lines, and I would fain anticipate myself by saying that in my opinion physical laws might find their most perfect expression as relations between these world-lines. . . . Thus also three-dimensional geometry becomes a chapter in four-dimensional physics.

This geometrical interpretation of space-time, which Einstein at first resisted (perhaps because Minkowski, the demanding teacher, had had harsh things to say to Einstein, the lazy student, in Zurich), he later embraced with passion in his general theory of curved space-time.

WORLD-LINES, LIGHT CONES AND CLOSED TIMELIKE CURVES

An explicit and fascinating use of the world-line imagery is in Robert Heinlein's very first published story, "Life-Line" which appeared in the August 1939 issue of *Astounding Science Fiction* and is reprinted in Volume 1 of Isaac Asimov's *The Great SF Stories* series. The story makes a clever analogy, comparing a world-line with a telephone cable: The beginning and end points in space-time for the world-line (birth and death) are associated with breaks (or faults) in a telephone cable. By sending an electrical test signal along the cable and measuring the time delay until the arrival of the echo produced by the discontinuity of the break, a technician can both detect and locate a fault in the cable. In the same manner, Heinlein's story gadget sends a signal of unspecified nature up and down a world-line and thus locates the birth and death points (which are the discontinuities in the world-line). Knowledge of the latter date, in particular, causes financial stress among life insurance companies, and an exploration of this tension is the fictional point of the story.

In his general theory, Einstein showed how the geometry of space-time can be either flat (in the no-gravity, special relativity case) or curved (involving gravity), and he did this not by verbal, philosophical handwaving but by writing mathematical equations— the famous *gravitational tensor field equations*. These equations are quite complicated and are notoriously difficult to solve in most cases, but in certain very special situations they have been solved. Those solutions show how mass-energy and space-time interact. As the popular shorthand phrase states, "Curved space-time tells matter how to move, and matter tells space-time how to curve."

Indeed, probably the most direct evidence for space-time is the curved orbits of planets as they travel around the sun. This becomes obvious, however, only after some pretty heavy-duty math, which we won't concern ourselves with in this book. Other evidence of curved space-time is that gravity bends light, a prediction made by Einstein and later confirmed by the 1919 eclipse in which observers witnessed starlight, just grazing the sun's surface, being bent. Other astrophysical mechanisms also bend light, but they are all frequency dependent. Only curved space-time can bend light in the way that is typically observed to occur, without chromatic dispersion.

At the microscopic, local level, general relativity has causality built in (which means no time travel to the past), but on larger scales (on the order of the distances between neighboring galaxies) things can be a good deal more complicated. Large-scale, curved space-time can (according to some solutions to the field equations) lead to violations of causality. That is, on a large scale, curved space-time may lead to time travel *to the past*.

In 1949, Einstein's friend, mathematician Kurt Gödel, found one such solution to the field equations at the Institute for Advanced Study, in Princeton. Gödel's equations describe the movement of matter not only through space, but also backward in time along what are called *closed timelike world-lines* in space-time. These world-lines are such that if a human traveled on one (always at less than the speed of light so that special relativity is never violated), she would see everything around her happening in normal causal order from moment to moment (e.g., the second hand on her wrist watch would tick clockwise into the future), but eventually the world-line would close back on itself and the traveler would find herself back in her own past. That is what the physics and the mathematics in Gödel's solution imply. (We'll return to Gödel's universe in chapter seven.) This solution is a rational basis for discussing time travel to the past, and for you to write science fiction (not fantasy) stories about time machines and time travel. Unlike the young hero in the opening quote to this chapter, we don't have to take the old scientist's word for it.

It is helpful in discussions about space-time to use what are called Minkowski space-time diagrams. These are plots of the space-time coordinates of a particle; Minkowski called the resulting curve the world-line of the particle. Such diagrams are most generally four-dimensional (three space axes and one time axis) and thus very hard to visualize (much less draw). The convention is to make do whenever possible with a simplified space-time that has just one space axis (the horizontal axis) and one time axis (the vertical axis).

As time progresses upward there is no change (i.e., the particle is "at rest") in space along the horizontal axis. For a particle at rest in an observer's frame of reference, the particle's space-time diagram is simply a vertical world-line. If, on the other hand, the particle is moving at a constant speed, then its world-line is a straight line that tilts away from the vertical. (The higher the speed, the more tilt.) Moreover, if the particle is accelerating with ever-increasing speed, then its world-line will curve away from the vertical. Figure 3.1 shows these three cases (I've assumed that each particle is at spatial location $x = x_0$ when the time is $t = 0$).

Straight (uncurved) world-lines represent unaccelerated particles; i.e., particles experiencing no forces. Such particles are said

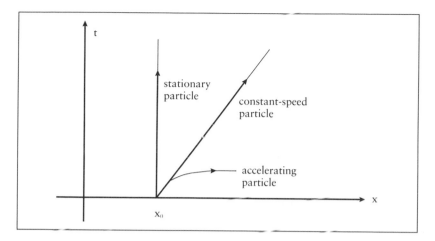

Fig. 3-1 World lines of three particles.

to be "in free-fall," as is the space shuttle in its orbit around the earth—astronauts float inside the cabin precisely because there are no forces on them. (If saying the shuttle is in "free fall" bothers you because it never actually falls to Earth, then think of the situation this way: The shuttle's orbital radius and speed are just such that as the shuttle *does* fall toward Earth, Earth's surface curves away by just the right amount to exactly compensate for the fall; i.e., the shuttle "falls endlessly" *around* the Earth.)

Free-fall world-lines are called space-time *geodesics*. In ordinary use, a path that joins two points on a surface with the minimum length is called a geodesic of that surface. On the surface of a sphere, for example, the geodesics are the great circles, formed by passing a plane through the two given points and the center of the sphere. These great circles (geodesic paths) are of much interest to the airlines, as their extreme property of minimum length allows pilots to minimize flight time and fuel cost of point-to-point flying.

In space-time, things are somewhat different. Space-time geodesics do indeed possess an extreme property, but rather than being a minimum, it is a maximum property. You need not worry about this for story writing, and I mention it only as an example of space-time's nonintuitive nature: Space-time diagrams can be misleading

because we tend to think of them as Euclidean geometry diagrams—they aren't.

It has become convention to draw space-time diagrams with the
speed of light as the reference speed; i.e., as unity ($c = 1$). Thus, all
other speeds are denoted by numbers less than one in accordance
with special relativity's demand that nothing can go faster than light.
This means that a distance of about 300,000 kilometers (186,000
miles) on the horizontal axis is represented by the same length as
one second on the vertical axis. That results in the world-line of a
photon being a straight line tilted away from the vertical axis by 45°.
Since photons can travel in both space directions (left or right) in
our simplified space-time, and since the speed of light is the limiting
speed (or so it is generally believed), we can represent the collection
of all possible world lines through a given point in space-time as all
those paths that don't tilt more than 45° away from the vertical in
either direction (as shown on the next page).

Now, a few definitions that are often useful for techtalk in time
travel stories. In Figure 3.3 (page 59), I have taken $x = 0$ at $t = 0$ for
all possible world-lines involving speeds below the speed of light.
Let us agree to call this point in space-time the *Here-Now*. Space-
time points (or events) in the upward region of the diagram, inside
the two limiting 45° lines, are in the future of the Here-Now. The
space-time points in the downward region of the diagram, again
inside the two limiting 45° lines, are in the past of the Here-Now.
These two regions form what is called the *light cone* at the Here-
Now because if we include a second space dimension, y, directed
vertical to the page, the upward and downward regions would be
cones.

CAUSALITY

We can draw a straight world-line from the Here-Now to any point
in its future light cone with a tilt of less than 45° away from the
vertical, which means a particle could travel from the Here-Now to
that future point at a speed less than that of light. Similarly, a particle
starting at any point in the past light cone could have reached the

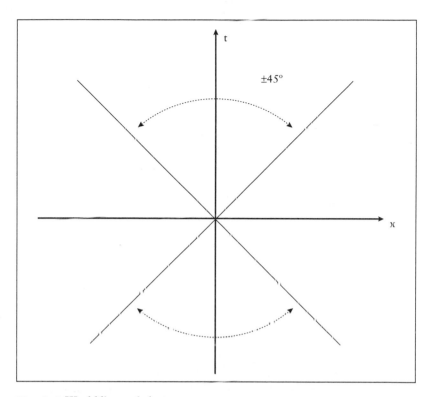

Fig. 3-2 World-lines of photons.

Here-Now by traveling, always, at less than the speed of light. Such world-lines, lying totally within the light cone, are called *timelike* because their projection onto the time axis is greater than their projection onto the space axis: They are "more like time" than space.

They are the world-lines of space-time points that are (at least potentially) causally linked. That is, a cause at a space-time point in the past cone could have had an effect on the event at the Here-Now, even though its influence always traveled at less than the speed of light. Also, a cause at the Here-Now could potentially affect an event at any point in the future light cone of the Here-Now.

Any point in the regions of space-time outside of the future and past light cones cannot be reached from the Here-Now except by world-lines that tilt, somewhere/when, at more than 45° away from the vertical. Such world-lines, which represent travel at a speed in

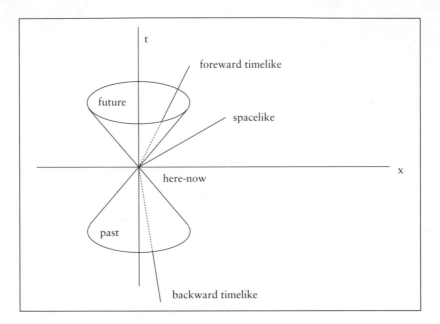

Fig. 3-3 A light cone with spacelike and timelike world-lines.

excess of that of light, are called *spacelike* because their projection onto the space axis is greater than their projection onto the time axis: They are "more like space" than time. It is impossible for these world-lines to connect causally linked events, and collectively they form the *Else-When* of the Here-Now.

It is very important to realize that every point in space-time has its own light cone, its own future and past and its own Else-When. These light cones overlap if one goes far enough into the past or future. If space-time point *B* is in the future light cone of space-time point *A*, then *A* is in the past light cone of *B*. There is nothing magical or mysterious about a space-time point *C* in the Else-When of the Here-Now, as for some other Here-Now *C* is in the associated light cone, and thus is either in the past or the future of that other Here-Now.

This imagery of the light cone is often useful in making seemingly abstract ideas appear almost transparent. For example, consider the ancient question: Can we predict the future? More specifically, can an observer predict her own future from perfect knowledge of her own past? The easy answer is "No, because quantum uncertainties prohibit perfect knowledge of even the present, much less the past." But suppose we ignore quantum mechanics and limit our question to a universe that obeys only classical physics (which includes special and general relativity)? Surprisingly (perhaps), the answer is still "no." Having perfect knowledge of your own past light cone doesn't include knowing the entire past. If you attempt to predict your own future (say one minute from now), there can be influences in your current Else-When that will arrive in the future (say, fifty-nine seconds from now) about which you presently *cannot* have any knowledge. Without that knowledge, you cannot predict with total certainty.

A space-time diagram does not always have to have future-directed world-lines. If a particle moves backward through time, assuming of course it is possible, then the diagram can show this movement by having the world-line double back on itself, as in Figure 3.4. In this example, the world-line curves back and comes arbitrarily close to itself. This is the world-line of a particle that visits itself in the past. Notice that the world-line does not actually cross or even just touch itself, as that would represent more than simply a visit—that would be a particle occupying the same spatial location, at the same time, as did its earlier self. That would be catastrophic.

The direction of the arrows on the world-line is always in the direction of the local future of the particle; e.g., if the particle is a human, then memories are formed in the direction of the arrows. The time traveler at **B** has more memories than she does at **A**, even though **A** and **B** are nearly identical points in space-time. There is a problem here, however, that the alert reader will have caught—it is impossible to draw such a double-backed world-line because in space-time it always tilts more than 45° away from the vertical; i.e., at least some portion of such a bent world-line will tilt outside of the local light cone, and that represents superluminal, faster-than-light travel, which violates special relativity. I'll return to the general issue of faster-than-light in more detail in chapter ten. For now, let me just say that one way to keep a bent-back world-line always subluminal is to tilt the light cones along the world-line relative to each other. As

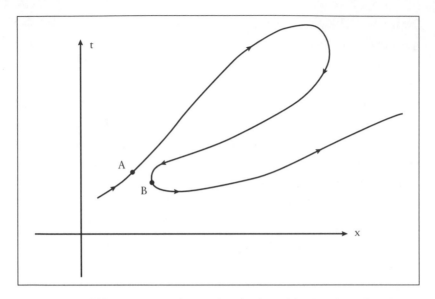

Fig. 3-4 World-line of a particle traveling backward in time from A to B.

shown in the last illustration, this is possible only in a space-time that is *curved*.

This is an illustration of how general relativity obeys special relativity locally, yet globally, in curved space-time, things are not so simple. In flat space-times, the light cones are globally aligned, but in curved space-times they are not. This detail makes time travel to the past possible. (Minkowski space-time is flat, so time travel to the past is impossible in it.)

On television, bent-back world-lines appeared in the time travel theory (a so-called "string theory") of *Quantum Leap*. In that theory, human lives are like pieces of string: One end is birth, the other is death, and every day of life is some point on the string between the two ends. Tying the ends together gives a loop in time, and if you squeeze the loop together "then each day of your life would touch another day." This poetic image explains why the show's time travel adventures were limited to within the traveler's own lifetime—but, alas, not a word on how to do it.

Curved space-time quickly showed up in pulp science fiction. In the October 1930 issue of *Amazing Stories*, Edmond Hamilton (one of the pioneering writers in science fiction pulp) published a sophisticated story, "The Man Who Saw the Future." In this tale, there are repeated references to Einstein and to other scholars of relativity. It tells the story of a young man who is hauled before the Inquisitor Extraordinary of the King of France to explain his mysterious disappearance from an open field and subsequent reappearance amid thunderclaps and in plain sight of many onlookers. As the story unfolds, we learn that the young man was transported five centuries into the future, from A.D. 1444 to 1944, by scientists working in twenty-fifth-century Paris. The thunderclaps were produced by space-time "rotations," as the air volumes of 1944 and 1444 were reversed. The classical minds of the Inquisition find this "explanation" preposterous, of course, and the first (involuntary) time traveler is burned at the stake as a sorcerer. Being a pioneer can be risky.

Like most technical developments, world-lines have gradually worked their way down in fictional literature to ever less sophisticated audiences. In Poul Anderson's "Little Monster," a story written for youngsters, a young boy asks his uncle-physicist how a time machine works. His uncle says, "Come back when you know tensor calculus and I'll explain to you about n-dimensional forces and the warping of world-lines."

ANTIMATTER AND TIME TRAVEL

World-lines bending back on themselves—and backwards time travel—have actually been around in physics (not just science fiction) since the 1940s. In a famous 1949 paper by the late Nobel Prize-winning Caltech physicist Richard Feynman, he suggests that a positron, appearing to us to be moving forward in time, is actually an electron traveling backward through time. (A positron is identical to an electron in every respect except for electrical charge. The electron carries a negative electronic charge, while the positron has the same amount of positive charge. The positron is the so-called antiparticle of the electron; i.e., if the electron is normal matter, then the positron is *antimatter*.)

In support of his time travel thesis, Feynman first asks us to

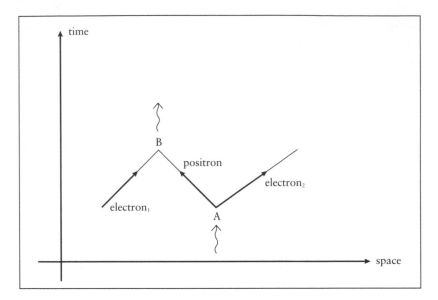

Fig. 3-5 Antimatter via backward time travel.

imagine the process shown in the space-time diagram in Figure 3.5. Gamma ray **A** spontaneously creates an electron-positron pair, with electron$_2$ moving off to some distant region. The positron soon meets with electron$_1$, resulting in mutual annihilation and the production of gamma ray **B**. This description involves three particles— each segment of the kinked line is a distinct particle.

Feynman said there is another way to look at this, however, and he gave a description using just one particle. According to Feynman, the kinked line in the figure is the world-line of a single electron. The middle segment is simply the electron traveling backward in time, so we must reverse the arrow on it.

There are two central questions at this point. First, why is a positron (with positive charge) moving backward in time mathematically equivalent to an electron (with negative charge) moving forward in time? The answer is that the reversal in charge sign is caused by the reversal of the electron's time direction, in accordance with the time-charge-parity theorem (about which much more can be found in my *Time Machines*). I mention this only to assure you that there is an explanation that practically all physicists find noncontroversial.

Far more controversial is the second question—what causes our single electron to suddenly start moving backward in time? It is recoiling from the emitted energy burst of gamma ray **B**. Just as momentum and space are complementary variables (conservation of momentum can actually be derived from the reasonable assumption that the laws of physics are the same in every direction of space), and just as a particle can reverse its direction of motion in space if it loses enough momentum, so too can a particle reverse its direction of motion in time if it loses enough energy. This follows because energy and time are another pair of complementary variables. That is, the conservation of energy can be derived from the assumption that the laws of physics are the same in both directions of time, an assumption that every known law of physics satisfies.

In the same way, the absorption of the energy of gamma ray **A** by the electron now recoiling backward in time causes a second recoil forward in time, creating the world-line of what we originally called electron$_2$. This reinterpretation of a kinked space-time diagram was described as follows in Feynman's own words: "It is as though a bombardier flying low over a road suddenly sees three roads, and it is only when two of them come together and disappear again that he realizes that he has simply passed over a long switchback in a single road."

Feynman's words were published in 1949, but he had first gotten hold of the idea of particles traveling backward in time in 1941. In an astonishing coincidence, as Feynman was thinking along these lines two science fiction writers came up with the same idea. Writing under the pen-name "Will Stewart," Jack Williamson and John W. Campbell (the editor of *Astounding Science Fiction*) identified anti-matter (what they called "contraterrene matter") with backward time travel in their story "Minus Sign" (*Astounding Science Fiction*, November 1942).

WHY WELLS'S TIME MACHINE COULDN'T WORK
It should now be clear that the only way a world-line can bend back on itself for a close encounter visit in curved space-time is for both *x* (space) and *t* (time) to change; i.e., the world-line of a particle that

remains fixed in space and reverses just its time direction runs into itself. This is why the classic time machine of H.G. Wells could not possibly work. Any real time machine must move through space as well as time (e.g., as does the DeLorean time car in the *Back to the Future* films, as does Superman in the first *Superman* (1978) movie when he flies faster than light back in time to save Lois from death, or even as does the otherwise ridiculous time machine in the 1962 movie *The Three Stooges Meet Hercules*). This point is so important, it deserves elaboration.

All of the "real" time machines that will be described later in this book (rotating cylinders, black holes, Gödel rockets, cosmic strings and space-time wormholes) require spatial movement. Wells's machine, however, does not move; it always remains in the Time Traveller's laboratory (or on the spot that was the laboratory) unless he or the Moorlocks push it about after a trip. Such so-called Wellsian time machines are common in science fiction (I'll admit to using one in my story "Newton's Gift," *Omni*, January 1979), but they really won't do for physicists. They have several troublesome problems (for an interesting list of dozens of them, see the article by Lafleur in the Bibliography), but let's just talk about the fatal "running into itself" problem.

Consider: There sits my time machine as I prepare for the first time journey ever, a trip back to the late Mesozoic era to hunt dinosaur. I load my Continental .600 with Nitro Express cartridges the size of bananas (this wonderful bit of imagery is inspired by L. Sprague de Camp's classic "A Gun for Dinosaur," a "must-read" for all science fiction writers of time travel), make sure my blood-proof boots are laced up tight, kiss my wife goodbye, and climb in. I pull the temporal displacement lever. Now, Wellsian-type time machines don't "jump over" time, but rather travel "through" time (see the Time Traveller's own description of how things looked to him, a description faithfully and spectacularly reproduced in the 1960 film). Therefore, the time machine will instantly collide with itself at the micromoment before I pull the lever.

This is not a simple bumping collision, but one in which atomic matter literally touches atomic matter as the two machines snuggle together in the same place at the same time, so the result is a nuclear reaction. The resulting destruction obviously introduces a nice paradox—if the nuclear reaction happens before I pull the lever (by definition the time machine has hit itself in the past), how did I manage to pull it? And if I don't pull it, then why is there a catastrophic detonation that reduces everything within a hundred-mile radius from the time machine to gamma rays powerful enough to penetrate, say, fifty feet of lead?

Think about this for a while, and I'll come back to it and other time travel paradoxes in chapter eight.

SUMMARY

In this chapter you've learned that it is Einstein's *general theory of relativity* that provides theoretical support to the possibility of time travel to the past. We have discussed the concepts of the *world-line*, the *light cone* centered on the Here-Now that separates the past from the future, and world-lines that curve or loop back on themselves in time to form *closed timelike* world-lines. You've also been introduced to *space-time diagrams* that illustrate the geometry of space-time, and you've seen how such diagrams show that space-time can't be flat if time travel is to be possible, i.e.; space-time must, somehow, be curved if a time machine is to exist. Finally, you've had a brief, first peek at a time travel paradox, in which a Wellsian (stationary) time machine crashes into itself in the past.

CHAPTER 4

Hyperspace

The three dimensions are all that there are.

Aristotle, from his circa 350 B.C. essay "On the Heavens."

Much of the modern literature on time machines and time travel is presented in terms of spaces with four, five or even more dimensions. Even if we reduce the count by one (for the nonspatial time dimension), we are still left with more than three dimensions, *hyperspace*. We shouldn't let the above epigram worry us too much, however, because Aristotle was pretty much a washout as a physicist—recall his famously wrong assertion that the heavier an object, the faster it will fall. His claim about the number of dimensions to space is not yet clearly a similar mistake, but I would bet that a sizeable number of modern physicists suspect it will eventually prove to be.

A fundamental biological-topological argument has been advanced for why space could not have less than three dimensions. In all of our common experiences, intelligent life is always found to occur as an aggregate of a vast number of elementary cells interconnected via electrical nerve fibers. Each such cell is connected to several others, not all immediate neighbors, by these fibers. If space had only one or two dimensions, then such highly interconnected cellular networks would be impossible, as the overlapping nerve fibers would intersect, resulting in their mutually shorting one another. Edwin Abbott's 1880 fantasy classic *Flatland*, then, is fatally flawed on a biological level.

It might be thought that the three-dimensionality of space is obvious since we use exactly three numbers to locate a position in space. To quote H.G. Wells, from his 1934 *Experiment in Autobiography*, "In the universe in which my brain was living in 1879, there was no nonsense about time being space or anything of that sort. There were three dimensions, up and down, fore and aft and right and left, and I never heard of a fourth dimension until 1884 or thereabout. Then I thought it was a witticism."

But why three dimensions, and not some other number? As the mystical Russian philosopher P.D. Ouspensky wrote, "By an *independent direction* we mean . . . a line lying at right angles to another line. Our geometry . . . knows only three such lines which lie simultaneously at right angles to one another and are not parallel to each other. Why are there only three and not ten or fifteen? This we do not know." In an 1888 talk to the Philosophical Society of Washington, however, the American scientist Simon Newcomb dismissed the view that space must necessarily be three-dimensional as an "old metaphysical superstition." (Newcomb is of particular interest in time-travel discussions because he is the only *real* person mentioned in Wells's *The Time Machine*.)

The idea of a fourth dimension is viewed by many as simpleminded nonsense. In his 1897 Presidential Address to the American Mathematical Society, Simon Newcomb declared, "The introduction of what is now very generally called hyper-space (sic), especially space of more than three dimensions, into mathematics, has proved a stumbling block to more than one able philosopher." Even Einstein got into this business of speaking of the spooky nature of hyperspace when he wrote: "The non-mathematician is seized by a mysterious shuddering when he hears of 'four-dimensional' things, by a feeling not unlike that awakened by thoughts of the occult."

To understand just how right Einstein was with his statement, consider the reaction (in 1929) of one philosopher to general relativity: "We have no doubt in our mind that nobody can understand it (the fourth dimension), including Einstein himself. The incomprehensibility of [the theory's assumptions] is due to their nature. They deal with the fourth dimension . . . and the reality of time and space. They can only be described by a mathematician's hypothesis or by religious faith." Who could really blame the skeptical philosopher— how could there actually be four spatial dimensions? After all, anybody can see there are exactly three spatial dimensions and that is simply that. For science fiction writers, however, the fourth dimension (and hyperspace, in general) is a major concept in its own right, and it plays an essential part in time travel, too.

FOLDED SPACE-TIME AND WORMHOLES

And just what is hyperspace? It is a space of higher dimension than the one we obviously live in. As already discussed, our universe appears to be a four-dimensional world called *space-time*. This four-dimensional world can, at least mathematically, be thought of as the boundary or surface of a five-dimensional hyperspace. In the remarkably sophisticated early pulp story by Miles J. Breuer, "The Gostak and the Doshes," originally published in a 1930 issue of *Amazing Stories*, an eccentric scientist exclaims, "A mathematical physicist lives in vast spaces . . . where space unrolls along a fourth dimension on a surface distended from a fifth."

This is entirely analogous to the way the two-dimensional space of the surface of a sphere bounds the three-dimensional space of the sphere itself. For the inhabitants of the 1983 book *Sphereland* (a clever extension of *Flatland*), their hyperspace is the interior of the sphere (excluding time) that the surface they live on bounds. For such beings, for example, there would be two ways to travel from one pole to the other—the usual way on the surface of the world, or the hyperspace route through the sphere along the polar diameter. By thinking of the sphere as an apple and of the hyperspace path as a tunnel through the apple, it has become popular to call all such shortcuts through any hyperspace, whatever its dimensions, *wormholes* (a term coined in the 1950s by the Princeton physicist John A. Wheeler). Even more poetically, I have seen wormholes referred to as "space-time subways." In chapter nine, I'll discuss the particular relationship between hyperspatial wormholes and time travel.

It is obvious, in the case of sphereland, that the hyperspace (or wormhole) path is shorter than the surface path. A common way to visualize such hyperspace shortcuts is to imagine the beginning and end points of a journey as points A and B in the two-dimensional surface of a piece of paper. Then imagine that the paper is folded to position A over B, perhaps even with A almost touching B. The distance from A to B through hyperspace (the three-dimensional space in which the folding takes place) is much shorter than the distance following the surface of the paper (normal space). This is the example used in G.O. Smith's "The Möbius Trail" (*Thrilling Wonder Stories*, December 1948), explaining the instantaneous "space-warp" (wormhole) teleportation device invented by the story's hero. This is still the most common fictional use of space-time wormholes, that of explaining faster-than-light travel by using the shorter (relative to normal space) distance separating the wormhole mouths. But this is changing, and the time (travel) properties of hyperspace wormholes are also rapidly becoming known to writers of science fiction.

The idea of folded hyperspace has broken free from science fiction and can be found in modern stories in other genres as well. For example, in the Stephen King story "Mrs. Todd's Shortcut" (from his 1985 collection *Skeleton Crew*), a woman keeps finding ever shorter ways to drive from Castle Rock, Maine, to Bangor. As the crow flies, it is 79 miles, but she gets the journey down to 67 and later to 31.6, miles. When doubted, she replies: "Fold the map and see how many miles it is then . . . it can be a little less than a straight line if you fold it a little, or it can be a lot less if you fold it a lot." The doubter remains unconvinced, and replies, "You can fold a map on paper, but you can't fold land." For our purposes here, the creation of wormholes in space-time will be made into time machines in chapter nine, so we have to actually imagine much more: the folding of four-dimensional space-time through a five-dimensional hyperspace.

SPACE AS THE FOURTH DIMENSION

German mathematician and astronomer August Möbius discovered one particularly fascinating attribute of hyperspace in 1827 by showing that any three-dimensional object can be converted into its mirror image by flipping it over through the fourth dimension; e.g., a left-handed glove can be made by pure geometry (no scissors, thread and needle required) into a precise copy of its right-handed mate. This wonderful idea has been used in fiction, of course (e.g., Wells's "The Plattner Story"). Such tales, which involve flipping humans over through the fourth dimension, have a literally fatal flaw that all science fiction writers today must know. Everything in the body would be reversed by such a flip, including the optically active organic molecules (discovered by Pasteur in 1848) which are involved in vital biological processes. These molecules, called *stereoisomers*, exist in two versions in nature (the left-handed and right-handed versions, if you will), but our bodies have developed the biological ability to use only one version. To be flipped through the fourth dimension would, for example, make some reversed stereoisomers unable to participate in the digesting of food, and we would starve to death.

This problem was first fictionally addressed in Arthur C. Clarke's 1946 story "Technical Error," where the solution was to flip the victim through the fourth dimension a second time. There is more to worry about with dimensional flipping than eating, however. Indeed, since everything flips, matter should become antimatter (this is a special case of the positron as an electron flipped over in time—recall chapter three), and Lewis Carroll was more correct than he could have imagined when he had Alice wonder, in *Through the Looking-Glass*, "Perhaps looking-glass milk isn't good to drink." Unless Alice is an anti-Alice, she and the anti-milk would have mutually become pure energy via a spectacular 100 percent efficient explosion.

In *Time Machines*, I give many examples of how early science fiction writers used the dramatic concept of hyperspace as four spatial dimensions in just about every imaginable way (always, it seems, with the stock character of a slightly batty professor), including surgery without cutting, robbing locked safe deposit boxes, and rescuing condemned criminals right off the scaffold by pulling them through the fourth dimension of space. One example that I didn't give in *Time Machines* shows how an early pulp writer nicely extended the basic idea of a fourth spatial dimension as being perpendicular to each of the three we see in our everyday world. As one character says in L.A. Eshbach's "The Time Conqueror" (*Wonder Stories*, July 1932), "Beyond the fourth there is a fifth dimension. . . . Eternity, I think you would call it. It is the line, the direction perpendicular to time."

Many years later, Isaac Asimov incorporated Eshbach's idea (and terminology) into his famous 1955 time travel novel *The End of Eternity*, in which the time police (called Eternals) oversee the endless centuries from a "place" outside of time (a part of hyperspace called Eternity). Harry Harrison did the same in his 1967 *The Technicolor Time Machine*, in which time travel takes place in a hyperspace called the "extratemporal continuum."

These are all time interpretations of hyperspace, of course, and somewhat premature in this book. I'll come back to it in later chapters.

SUMMARY

In this chapter you've read of the *hyperspace* concept, a space with four (or more) dimensions. Four-dimensional space-time is a special case of hyperspace. One aspect of such spaces, of particular interest to a writer of time travel stories, is the *wormhole*. Wormholes are predicted to exist by general relativity, and they are shortcuts between two points in everyday three-dimensional space, taken through the hyperspace of which the three-dimensional space is part. Wormholes are important to science fiction writers because, as I will show you in chapter nine, they can theoretically be made into time machines.

CHAPTER 5

Time as the Fourth Dimension

The shadow by my finger cast
Divides the future from the past:
Before it, sleeps the unborn hour,
In darkness, and beyond thy power:
Behind its unreturning line,
The vanished hour, no longer thine:
One hour alone is in thy hands,
The now *on which the shadow stands.*

"The Sun-Dial at Wells College" by Henry Van Dyke, 1904.

Time as the fourth dimension of space-time, (rather than that dimension being spatial in nature) is the current idea today. As with the spatial interpretation, the time view is an old one, which can be traced back to at least the eighteenth century. There is, in fact, a famous passage dating to 1751, in the writings of the French mathematician Jean le Rond D'Alembert (1717–1783), that shows just how old such speculations are: "I have said [that it is] not possible to imagine more than three dimensions. A clever acquaintance of mine believes, however, that duration could be regarded as a fourth dimension; that idea can be contested, but it seems to me that it has some merit, if only that of novelty."

It wasn't until a curious letter appeared in *Nature* during 1885, however, that the concept of time as the fourth dimension was mentioned seriously in an English-language scientific journal. The author, mysteriously signing himself only as "S.", began by writing, "What is the fourth dimension? . . . I [propose] to consider Time as a fourth dimension. . . . Since this fourth dimension cannot be introduced into space, as commonly understood, we require a new kind of space for its existence, which we may call time-space." Who was this prophetic writer? Nobody knows.

The idea of time as the fourth dimension entered the popular mind ten years later, around 1894-1895, with the first of H.G. Wells's so-called scientific romances, *The Time Machine*. Twenty years after this pioneer use of time in literature, science fiction writers took the idea as the basis for one of their most popular subgenres. For example, Murray Leinster was quick to capitalize on time as the fourth dimension; his very first published story, "The Runaway Skyscraper" (which appeared in a 1919 issue of *Argosy* magazine), tells the incredible tale of how a Manhattan skyscraper and its 2,000 occupants' trip several thousand years backward in time when the building's foundation slips (in some unexplained way) along the fourth dimension.

The scientific sophistication of the story is primitive, with just one of the logical flaws being a vivid description of the time travelers living normal, forward-in-time lives even as their wristwatches run backward. Indeed, when Hugo Gernsback reprinted the tale in one of the early issues of *Amazing Stories*, a reader complained about this very point. Gernsback felt compelled to defend the story in his November 1926 editorial "Plausibility in Scientifiction" (see the opening to chapter one), but he could muster only a weak rebuttal based on an author's right to "poetic license." Perhaps in 1926, but today such a slip would bring hoots of laughter down on a writer's head.

Using an interesting dual interpretation of the fourth dimension is Arthur C. Clarke's "Technical Error," the story of an electrical engineer who is caught in the middle of an enormous electromagnetic field surge produced by a short circuit in a power plant. As a physicist later explains to the utility's shaken board of directors: "It now appears that the unheard-of current, amounting to millions of amperes . . . must have produced a certain extension into four dimensions . . . I have been making some calculations and have been able to satisfy myself that a 'hyperspace' about ten feet on a side was, in fact, generated: a matter of some ten thousand quartic—not cubic!—feet. Nelson was occupying that space. The sudden collapse of the field [when the overload breakers finally cut the circuit] caused the rotation of the space."

Being rotated through four-dimensional space has inverted the unlucky Nelson (recall Alice and her looking-glass milk from the last chapter) and, to bring him back to normal, he must be flipped again. The physicist brushes aside a question about the fourth dimension as time, asserting the whole issue is simply one of space. Poor Nelson is again subjected to a stupendous power overload—only now he disappears. Too late, the physicist realizes that the fourth dimension is (in this story) both space and time. Nelson, who has been spatially flipped once more, has also been temporally displaced into the future (where he rematerializes inside a thousand-ton, fifty million horse-power generator). Clarke's final sentence is masterful in delivering its chilling message (remember what I said would happen if a time machine ran into itself in the past?): "The power station was invisible beyond the foothills . . . but its site was clearly marked by the vast column of debris that was slowly rising against the bleak light of the dawn."

Modern physics does indeed think of time as the fourth dimension, but for many powerful thinkers, from ancient times right up to our times, it hasn't been entirely clear just *what* time is, or even if it is real. The mystery of time was well-captured by R.H. Hutton, the literary editor of the *Spectator,* in his 1895 review of Wells's *The Time Machine*: "The story is based on that rather favorite speculation of modern metaphysicians which supposes *time* to be at once the most important of the conditions of organic evolution, and the most misleading of subjective illusions . . . and yet Time is so purely subjective a mode of thought, that a man of searching intellect is supposed to be able to devise the means of traveling in time as well as in space, and visiting, so as to be contemporary with, any age of the world or future, so as to become as it were a true 'pilgrim of eternity'."

Novelist Israel Zangwill wrote a similar but much more analytic review of Wells's novel for the *Pall Mall Magazine*. Zangwill was the only Victorian reviewer to attempt a scientific analysis of time travel. While he thought Wells's effort was a "brilliant little romance," Zangwill also thought the time machine, "much like the magic carpet of *The Arabian Nights*," was "an amusing fantasy." Zangwill continued with what even then was a common idea about a way one might, at least in principle, look backward in time: You could travel far out into space by going faster than light, stop, and then watch the light from the past catch up with you. Note this was 1895, ten years before Einstein and the limitations of special relativity.

In this way, Zangwill wrote, one could watch "the Whole Past of the Earth still playing itself out." Early pulp writers found the idea of looking backward in time with delayed light to be a particularly romantic one; e.g., D.D. Sharp's "Faster Than Light" (*Marvel Science Stories*, February 1939). In this tale a scientist loses his wife to a rival, who kidnaps her and escapes in a faster-than-light rocketship headed for parts unknown. After years of searching for them with his own brilliant invention of the "ampliscope" (several quantum leaps beyond the telescope), the anguished scientist finally locates the couple skipping from planet to planet, light years distant. His only pleasure, then, is to use his own faster-than-light craft to outrun the light-images of his lost love and to watch them over and over. Eventually, he comes to understand the futility of it all. As the last line of the story says, "It would be senseless, I knew, chasing on and on after yesterdays." The science is pretty bad (what would really happen to a faster-than-light rocketship is discussed in chapter nine), but the emotion goes a long way to overcoming that shortcoming, and in my opinion it is, even nearly sixty years later, a nice little tale.

CIRCULAR, LINEAR AND HELICAL TIME

A different way to look backward in time is found in antiquity; the idea of looking forward in time, a concept that assumes time is a closed loop. Plato (circa 400 B.C.) thought of time as having a beginning, but his conception of time did not extend into the indefinite future (which is the modern view). Rather, he visualized it curving back on itself; that is, as circular time. This was a reasonable reflection of nature, with the seemingly endless repetitions of the seasons, the unvarying alternation of night and day, and the rotation of the planets in the sky. Whatever might be observed today would, it seemed obvious, happen again in the future. This view of time has a powerful, ancient visual symbol: The Worm Ouroborous or World Snake that eats its own tail endlessly. Circular time, with its closed topology, was favorably presented in Stephen Hawking's famous book *A Brief History of Time*, in which he concludes there is no need for God. Hawking arrived at this position because in circular time there is no first event, and hence no need for a first cause. As you can imagine, many theologians have taken issue with Hawking on this.

A close cousin to circular time is helical or spiral time, an idea popular in early science fiction time travel tales. Typical is R.H. Wilson's "A Flight Into Time" (*Wonder Stories,* February 1931), in which a time traveler suddenly finds himself not in 1933, but in 2189. His situation is explained to him thus: "[T]he time stream is curved helically in some higher dimension. In your case, a still further distortion brought two points of the coil into contact, and a sort of short circuit threw you into the higher curve."

Helical time offers a nice "way out" to one of the classical objections to time travel. As Arthur C. Clarke wrote in his essay "About Time" (included in his book *Profiles of the Future*), "the most convincing argument against time travel is the remarkable scarcity of time travelers. However unpleasant our age may appear to the future, surely one would expect scholars and students to visit us, if such a thing were possible at all [just like the time-traveling historian in Connie Willis's 1992 novel *Doomsday Book*, who visits the fourteenth century]. Though they might try to disguise themselves, accidents would be bound to happen—just as they would if we went back to imperial Rome with cameras and tape recorders concealed under our nylon togas. Time traveling could never be kept secret for long." Indeed, in J. McDevitt's "Time's Arrow," as a skeptic explains this very concern to a would-be time machine inventor, "If it [time travel] *could* be done, someone will eventually learn how. If that happens, history would be littered with tourists. They'd be everywhere. They'd be on the *Santa Maria*, they'd be at Appomattox with Polaroids, they'd be waiting outside the tomb, for God's sake, on Easter morning."

According to this argument (which you'll see again, in chapter eleven, as one of Hawking's reasons for thinking time travel impossible), from the moment after the first time machine is constructed, through all the rest of civilization, there would be countless historians (to say nothing of weekend sightseers) who would want to visit every important historical event in recorded history. They might each come from a different time in the future, but all would arrive at destinations crowded with temporal colleagues—crowds for which there is no historical evidence. Helical time offers an explanation for this puzzle. As Clarke wrote in his essay about the problem of missing time travelers, "Some science-fiction writers have tried to get round this difficulty by suggesting that Time is a spiral; though we may not be able to move along it, we can perhaps hop from coil to coil, visiting so many millions of years apart that there is no danger of embarrassing collisions between cultures. Big game hunters from the future may have wiped out the dinosaurs, but the age of *Homo sapiens* may lie in a blind region which they cannot reach."

THE DIRECTION OF TIME

If time is a dimension, it would seem reasonable to ask if it has direction. And, in fact, the answer seems too obvious: Of course time has direction; everybody knows it flows from past to future. There is a curious language problem, however, because we also like to say that the present recedes into the past, suggesting flow in the opposite direction, from future to past. Given this uncomfortable situation of snarled syntax, can we at least distinguish past from future, whichever way time might flow? Even this simplified question is not so simple to answer. The central debate in physics and philosophy is between *objective time* (the idea that time really does flow), and *mind-dependent time* (the belief that time flow is an illusion). So, from here on, when I write of "time flowing," keep in mind that the meaning of those words (if anything) is still a pretty big mystery. The idea of time flowing is a popular one, nonetheless, and it repeatedly appears in the time-travel literature as the "river of time" (or the "ocean of time").

One of the earliest (if not *the* earliest) treatments of the flowing time in science fiction is due to Caltech math professor Eric Temple Bell. His famous novel *The Time Stream* began to appear in December 1931 as a serial in *Wonder Stories,* under the pen name "John Taine." Strong evidence exists that this work, in which Bell made great use of time as a flowing stream in which one could swim into the future or the past, was actually written long before its publication (perhaps as early as July 1921), but he had been unable to find a publisher because of its then-startling concept.

By 1931, however, others had found a more receptive audience, with pulp editors eager for new stories in the new genre, and they beat Bell into print. For example, the early pulp story by E.A. Manley and W. Thode, "The Time Annihilator" (*Wonder Stories,* November 1930), used the watery image of time to play with its erosive nature in a dramatic way. As two time travelers speed into the future to rescue a friend, one of them describes the scene for us: "We huddled together in the whirling time-girdling machine, cutting through the years as a ship's prow breasts surging waves. I could not help but think of the years as waves, beating in endless succession on the sands of eternity. They wore all away before them with pitiless attrition. Time seemed to eat all with dragon jaws."

Manley and Thode's prose was taken a step further in J. Wyndham's "Wanderers of Time" (*Wonder Stories,* March 1933), a story in which a large number of time travelers from all across time find themselves stranded at precisely the same place. One of them offers his theory of what has caused this remarkable coincidence— they all have faulty time machines, like faulty boats, and have hit the same snag on the "river of time." As he explains, "You may turn boats adrift on a river at many points, and they will all collect to-gether at the same serious obstacle whether they have traveled a hundred miles or two miles. We are now at some period where the straight flow of time has been checked—perhaps it is even turning back on itself . . . we have struck some barrier and been thrown up like so much jetsam."

ENTROPY AS AN ARROW OF TIME

The idea of time having a direction, pointing like a sign from past to future, is called the *arrow* of time. Many attempts have been made, since the middle of the nineteenth century to explain why time has an arrow. These arrow explanations go under a variety of names, including the cosmological arrow (the expansion of the universe), the electromagnetic arrow (radio waves travel into the future), and the psychological arrow (we remember the past, not the future). The arrow that has found the most use in science fiction, however, is the so-called thermodynamic arrow (heat energy flows from hot to cold), otherwise known as *entropy.*

It was the Englishman A.S. Eddington who gave the eloquent name of the "arrow of time" to the observed asymmetric nature of time's direction from past to future, and it was Eddington who popularized entropy as the explanation for the arrow. This explana-tion is based on the second law of thermodynamics, which states that a measure of the internal randomness or disorder (*entropy*) of any closed system (one free of all external influences) continually evolves toward the condition of maximum disorder, the condition called *thermodynamic equilibrium.* Indeed, so striking is the in-crease of entropy with time, in a macroscopically large system, that it has come to be thought of as defining the direction of time, pointing toward the future.

The steady increase in entropy is an often-observed phenomenon in the everyday world. A drop of ink in a glass of water, for example, spreads out in an expanding cloud that we never see collapse backward into a drop; a long rod of metal, initially hotter at one end than the other, evolves toward a constant temperature along its entire length. We never see a uniformly warm rod spontaneously begin to cool at one end and grow hot at the other. A hot bath grows cool. In all of these cases, the end state (the future) represents greater internal randomness or molecular disorder than does the beginning state (the past).

Low entropy was in the past; high entropy will be in the future. The increase of entropy defines a direction to time, and so entropy has come to be called the thermodynamic arrow of time. More correctly, it should be called the probabilistic (or statistical) arrow of time because there can be fluctuations in a system's evolution creating a temporal decrease in entropy. All we can say is that for macroscopically sized systems, even small fluctuations in entropy are most unlikely.

These statements are all accepted today as being true as far as they go. But there are a couple of puzzles here, too, ones that have been used by science fiction writers and that still have, I think, a lot of mileage left in them. The first puzzle, the so-called *reversibility paradox*, is based on the fact that the classical equations of physics work just as well with time running in either direction. Every known equation for a fundamental law of physics makes as much sense with "$-t$" as it does with "t." So why don't things go backward as described in Philip K. Dick's very strange, very brilliant novel *Counter-Clock World*? One nineteenth-century answer to this paradox is that a world could run backward if initial conditions are suitable; e.g., if all the velocity vectors of every particle in an equilibrium state are reversed, then the system will unwind backward in time toward its original nonequilibrium condition. A system in thermodynamic equilibrium, the state of greatest entropy, could evolve toward a state of low entropy. It was even suggested that such might be the case for regions in our own universe; i.e., there might be beings in a world somewhere who experience time running counter to our experience (shades of Dick's novel).

The *recurrence paradox* is something entirely different from reversibility; it is based on an 1890 theoretical result due to the great French mathematician Henri Poincaré. Motivated by the question of the stability of the motion of three masses governed by Newton's laws of mechanics (the famous "three body problem"), Poincaré showed that under very general conditions any fixed-volume system will return infinitely often and with arbitrarily little error to almost every previous state. If you wait long enough, implies Poincaré's theorem, Pearl Harbor will happen again, and again, and again and. . . . In 1896 the German mathematician Ernst Zermelo used this result (called the "eternal return" by philosophers) to claim that there could be no truly irreversible processes, and thus he cast doubt on the inexorable increase of entropy as really defining the arrow of time.

In fiction, the idea of a repetition of human affairs preceded Poincaré with M. Clarke's 1872 story "Human Repetends." (In mathematics, if a fraction has an endlessly repeating decimal expansion the repeating part is called the *repetend*.) Of course, it seems as though we could never know of the event of a recurrence, as the state of all conceivable records (geological evidence, memories, books, films, and so on) would also recur as part of the physical state of the universe. And those records could contain no knowledge of the recurrence because it had not happened "yet." This very point is, in fact, the logical flaw in the 1993 time loop film *Groundhog Day*.

Even for very small systems, such as a mere handful of molecules, the recurrence time is extremely large—on the order of millions of billions of years—as discussed by J.M. Blatt in a *Scientific American* article. And for the entire universe itself, the recurrence time is simply incomprehensible—mathematicians call one followed by a hundred zeros a *googol* (an absolutely enormous number, far larger than the number of raindrops that have fallen on the entire

Earth over its entire history), and the recurrence time for the universe (in years) has been estimated to be one followed by a googol of zeros (a so-called *googolplex* of years, which is immensely longer than a mere googol of years).

It didn't take long for science fiction to incorporate entropy into time travel. In F.B. Long's "Temporary Warp" (*Astounding Stories,* August 1937), for example, the inventor of the amazing "warp gun" explains, "The stupendous distortion of the warp may actually bring about a sort of kink in space-time, and result in a reversal of entropy;" when the gun is fired, however, a woman who is hit by the warp ages seventy years in seconds (which is, of course, precisely the wrong effect).

There are many other stories from pulp fiction that used entropy, but one is simply so awful (funny) I have to tell you about it here. In P. Cross's melodramatic "Prisoner of Time" (*Super Science Stories,* May 1942), Bryce Field, "a master-scientist, a demon, cruel, ruthless," uses the entropy interpretation of the arrow of time for revenge. Field is rejected in love by the lovely Lucy Grantham. Her lack of enthusiasm is perhaps understandable, as he is described as having "a lean-jawed, sunken-eyed" appearance, with "lank, untidy hair sprawled across his massive forehead." Lucy tells him at one point, "I could never love you; you are too clever, too brilliantly scientific."

Before we are more than a page or two into this unintentionally hilarious tale, Bryce has Lucy strapped to a steel table in an underground cave-laboratory. Then he tells her fate: "You are going on a long journey, my dear. So long a journey that even I, master-scientist, do not know when it will end. A journey into the future— alone! . . . You, Lucy, shall be the victim of entropy! . . . I have discovered how to make a [globe] of non-time. Entropy will be halted [the master-scientist really should have said that the *change* in entropy will be halted] . . . You will be plunged into an eternal 'now.' " And so the mad Doctor Field throws the switch on the wall of his "instrument-littered" cave on July 17, 1941, and Lucy remains "suspended" in time until the outside world reaches August 9, 2450.

That is the day she is dug up by "big and muscular" engineer Clem Bradley and his "square-jawed" sidekick Buck Cardew, who use a "warp in space-time" to release Lucy from her "globe of non-time." What horrible stuff!

Poul Anderson used entropy in a similar but vastly more scientific way in his "Time Heals," which describes a scientist's discovery of "a field in which entropy was held level." As Anderson explains, "An object in such a field could not experience any time flow—for it, time would not exist"; this is because time flow is change in entropy, and the change of a constant is zero. Anderson speculates in this tale about how such a field could have fantastic home uses ("Imagine cooking a chicken dinner, putting it in the field, and taking it out piping hot whenever needed, maybe twenty years hence!"), but its real use in the story is as a stasis generator for preserving fatally ill people until medical science has learned how to cure their diseases. This is simply a high-tech method of suspended animation, of time traveling into the future by a sort of sleeping. The gadget that does this is called (somewhat sinisterly) the "Crypt." Anderson tells us that it also makes a great bomb shelter because "not even an atom bomb could penetrate a stasis field." The reason for this is intriguing: "The field requires a finite time in which to collapse— only there is no time in it." The interior of the non-changing entropy of the Crypt is, literally, a region in which time's arrow has fallen to the ground, motionless.

Without question, however, Robert Silverberg is the science fiction writer who has embraced the relationship between entropy and time travel with the most enthusiasm. For example, when newspapers from the future appear on people's doorsteps in "What We Learned From This Morning's Newspaper," the initial astonishment is replaced by puzzlement as the papers rapidly disintegrate. We are told it is the result of "entropic creep." The explanation continues, informing us that it is sort of like a strain in a geological fault (Silverberg lives in Oakland, California, now and then the site of large to huge earthquakes, and it isn't surprising that he uses this particular imagery): "Entropy, you know, is the natural tendency of everything in nature to come apart at the seam as time goes along. These newspapers must be subject to unusually strong entropic strains because of their anomalous position out of their proper place in time."

And in his "In Entropy's Jaws," Silverberg uses the randomness that underlies entropy. The story's central character is a telepathic "Communicator" who is burned-out by an information overload while mentally linking two clients. He becomes "unstuck in time," as does Billy Pilgrim in Kurt Vonnegut's *Slaughter-House Five*. Like Pilgrim, Silverberg's character starts oscillating, wildly and uncontrollably, back and forth between past and future. He is literally masticated by the teeth of time. The play on entropy and the job of Communicator is clear (entropy plays a central role in the mathematics of information theory), and Silverberg's character is caught "in entropy's jaws." Silverberg is clearly fascinated by the idea of swinging forward and backward through time, and has repeated it in his appropriately titled 1987 novel *Project Pendulum*.

SUMMARY

This chapter has introduced you to the time interpretation of the fourth dimension, as popularized in Wells's *The Time Machine*. The modern view of time's topology is that it is linear, with time stretched out like a taut string from past to future, but other possibilities, such as *circular* and *helical* time, have been used in science fiction. In physics, too, Stephen Hawking has expressed his willingness to embrace circular time. We discussed the idea of time having various arrows pointing in the direction of the future, with emphasis on the thermodynamic arrow (the internal chaos or *entropy* of a system tends to increase with increasing time). The entropy arrow was illustrated with some examples from time travel fiction, along with the associated paradoxes of reversibility (history running backwards) and recurrence (history repeating).

CHAPTER 6

The Block Universe

And now he has preceded me briefly in bidding farewell to this strange world. This signifies nothing. For us believing physicists, the distinction between past, present and future is only an illusion, even if a stubborn one.

Albert Einstein, in a letter dated March 21, 1955, to the children of his dearest friend Michele Besso, upon Besso's death.

In a little known, yet quite erudite essay published in a 1920 issue of the British science journal *Nature,* just after the first experimental verification of general relativity (the bending of starlight by the sun's gravity), an anonymous author presented an optical analogy to help those who thought relativity a mere "mathematical joke." Signing himself only as "W.G.," the writer included the following fascinating passage:

> Some thirty or more years ago [it was forty] a little *jeu d'esprit* was written by Dr. Edwin Abbott entitled "Flatland." . . . Dr. Abbott pictures intelligent beings whose whole experience is confined to a plane, or other space of two dimensions, who have no faculties by which they can become conscious of anything outside that space and no means of moving off the surface on which they live. He then asks the reader, who has

consciousness of the third dimension, to imagine a sphere descending upon the plane of Flatland and passing through it. How will the inhabitants regard this phenomenon? They will not see the approaching sphere and will have no conception of its solidity. They will only be conscious of the circle in which it cuts their plane. This circle, at first a point, will gradually increase in diameter, driving the inhabitants of Flatland outward from its circumference, and this will go on until half the sphere has passed through the plane, when the circle will gradually contract to a point and then vanish, leaving the Flatlanders in undisturbed possession of their country. . . . Their experience will be that of a circular obstacle gradually expanding or growing, and then contracting, and they will attribute to *growth in time* what the external observer in three dimensions assigns to motion in the third dimension. Transfer this analogy to a movement of the fourth dimension through three-dimensional space. Assume the past and future of the Universe to be all depicted in four-dimensional space and visible to any being who has consciousness of the fourth dimension. If there is motion of our three-dimensional space relative to the fourth dimension, all the changes we experience, and assign to the flow of time will be due simply to this movement, the whole of the future as well as the past always existing in the fourth dimension.

W.G.'s words are a clear and unequivocal statement of the so-called *block universe* concept of Minkowski's four-dimensional space-time, of reality as a once-and-forever entity. We can actually find the block universe idea in fiction before Minkowski. Consider, for example, G.C. Eggleston's 1875 story "The True Story of Bernard Poland's Prophecy," the tale of a man who sees his own death in the American Civil War, years in the future. As Bernard says to his unnamed friend (the narrator):

"Do you know," said Bernard, presently, "I sometimes think prophecy isn't so strange a thing . . . I really see no reason why any earnest man may not be able to foresee the future, now and then . . ."

"There is reason enough to my mind," I replied, "in the fact that future events do not exist, as yet, and we can not know that which is not, though we may shrewdly guess it sometimes . . ."

"Your argument is good, but your premises are bad, I think," replied my friend, . . . his great, sad eyes looking solemnly into mine.

"How so?" I asked.

"Why, I doubt the truth of your assumption, that future events do not exist as yet . . . Past and Future are only divisions of time, and do not belong at all to eternity. . . . To us it must be past or future with reference to other occurrences. But is there, in reality, any such thing as a past or a future? If there is an eternity, it is and always has been and always must be. But time is a mere delusion . . . To a being thus in eternity, all things are, and must be, present. *All things that have been, or shall be, are.*"

The origin of the specific term *block universe* is generally cited to be the Oxford philosopher Francis Herbert Bradley (1846–1924), who in his 1883 book *Principles of Logic* wrote: "We seem to think that we sit in a boat, and are carried down the stream of time, and that on the bank there is a row of houses with numbers on the doors. And we get out of the boat, and knock at the door of number 19, and, re-entering the boat, then suddenly find ourselves opposite 20, and, having then done the same, we go on to 21. And, all this while, the firm fixed row of the past and future stretches in a block behind us, and before us." The house numbers would seem to be Bradley's way of referring to the centuries. Notice that this statement was written twelve years before *The Time Machine*, and it preceded Minkowski by a quarter-century.

The block universe concept eventually made an impression on popular culture. For example, in a 1928 New York stage play, "Berkeley Square," the action alternately takes place in the years

1784 and 1928. To explain how this can be, the character who is doing the time traveling says to another, with words much like those of Bradley:

> Suppose you are in a boat, sailing down a winding stream. You watch the banks as they pass you. You went by a grove of maple trees, upstream. But you can't see them now, so you saw them in the *past*, didn't you? You're watching a field of clover now; it's before your eyes at this moment, in the *present*. But you don't know yet what's around the bend in the stream there ahead of you; there may be wonderful things, but you can't see them until you get around the bend, in the *future*, can you?

Then, after this prologue about the stream of time, comes the block universe idea:

> Now remember, *you're* in the boat. But *I'm* up in the sky above you, in a plane. I'm looking down on it all. I can see *all at once* the trees you saw upstream, the field of clover that you see now, and what's waiting for you, around the bend ahead! *All at once!* So the past, present and future of the man in the boat are all *one* to the man in the plane.

And then comes a theological conclusion: "Doesn't that show how all Time must really be one? Real Time — real Time is nothing but an idea in the mind of God!" Pretty deep stuff for the New York night crowd, don't you think?

In a famous philosophical paper by an advocate of the block-universe interpretation of reality, D.C. Williams stated "I . . . defend the view of the world . . . which treats the totality of being, of facts, or of events as spread out eternally in the dimension of time as well as the dimensions of space. Future events and past events are by no means present events, but in a clear and important sense they do exist, now and forever, as rounded and definite articles of the world's furniture."

This is pretty nifty prose, but in an even more famous essay published the same year (1951), Williams really made clear his belief

in the passage of time as a myth. He did so with the following astonishing words, ones that I think should send tingles down the backs
of all science fiction fans (and writers): "It is then conceivable,
though doubtless physically impossible, that one four-dimensional
area of the time part of the manifold be slewed around at right angles
to the rest, so that the time order of that area, as composed by its
interior lines of strain and structure, runs parallel with a spatial
order in its environment. It is conceivable, indeed, that a single
whole human life should lie thwartwise of the manifold, with its
belly plump in time, its birth at the east and its death in the west, and
its conscious stream running alongside somebody's garden path."

Now, I am willing to admit that Williams wrote that wonderful
passage mostly for effect, but I ask you—what, if anything, does it
mean? It is marvelous to read, but it remains totally mysterious. It
should come as no surprise that Williams originally read that passage at a meeting of the Metaphysical Society of America, and not
at a gathering of the American Physical Society. But it was perhaps
not without impact in areas outside of metaphysics—such as in science fiction. Consider, for example, Gene Wolfe's story "The Rub-
ber Bend," which reads as if Williams's paper was its direct inspiration. This is a tale in which a scientist discovers how to bend his
perception of the four dimensions so as to view verticality as duration, and duration as verticality. Thus, while sitting down he is in
October, but when he stands up he is in November.

Despite the enthusiastic embrace of the block universe by
Williams and many other philosophers (Einstein, too—take another
look at the quote opening this chapter), there have been those who
have been harsh in their criticism of Minkowski's space-time. The
major philosophical problem with the block universe interpretation
of four-dimensional space-time is that it appears to be fatalism disguised as physics. It seems to be a mathematician's denial of free
will dressed up in geometry. The Minkowski block universe is fatalistic, and you should keep the distinction between determinism and
fatalism clear in your mind; they are *not* the same. Determinism
says that if you do *A* then *B* will happen, but if you do *C* then *D* will

happen. That is, effects follow deterministically from causes, but you still have a choice on what cause to introduce. Fatalism, however, says you *will* do *A* and thus only *B* can possibly happen, *and* that you have no choice *but* to do *A*.

The late philosopher Hans Reichenbach has a charming little story in his 1956 book *The Direction of Time* that vividly demonstrates the compelling need in many humans to deny a fatalistic world:

> In a moving picture version of *Romeo and Juliet*, the dramatic scene was shown in which Juliet, seemingly dead, is lying in the tomb, and Romeo, believing she is dead, raises a cup containing poison. At this moment an outcry from the audience was heard: "Don't do it!" We laugh at the person who . . . forgets that the time flow of a movie is unreal, is merely the unwinding of a pattern imprinted on a strip of film. Are we more intelligent than this man when we believe that the time flow of actual life is different? Is the present more than our cognizance of a predetermined pattern of events unfolding itself like an unwinding film?

Most people in the Western world would answer *yes* to Reichenbach's question. Most such people, for example, find Khayyam's *Rubaiyat* to be a beautiful poem, but reject its fatalistic message: "And the first Morning of Creation wrote/What the Last Dawn of Reckoning shall read."

Besides fatalism, another reason for the stinging words of critics is, it seems that things don't happen in Minkowski's block universe—they just are; there seems to be no temporal process of *becoming* in Minkowski's space-time. Everything is already there and, as what we perceive as the passage of time occurs, we become ever more conscious of Minkowski's world-points (or *events*) that lie on our individual world-lines. Hermann Weyl (1885–1955), a German mathematical physicist who in his last years was a colleague of Einstein and Gödel at the Institute for Advanced Study in Princeton, expressed this view (in his 1949 book *Philosophy of Mathematics and Natural Science*) in words that have since become famous:

The objective world simply *is*, it does not *happen*. Only to the gaze of my consciousness, crawling upward along the life line of my body [Minkowski's world-line], does a section of the world [i.e., space-time] come to life as a fleeting image in space which continuously changes in time [i.e., the now or present]."

Now, after reading that, recall Wells's time traveler's speech to his friends:

There is no difference between Time and any of the three dimensions of Space except that our consciousness moves along it . . . here is a portrait of a man at eight years old, another at fifteen, another at seventeen, another at twenty-three, and so on. All these are evidently sections, as it were, Three-Dimensional representations of his Four-Dimensional being, *which is a fixed and unalterable thing* [my emphasis]."

This was written, remember, in 1895, thirteen years before Minkowski and his world-lines, and of course decades before Weyl's famous quote.

The block universe concept appeared very early in pulp science fiction. In F. Flagg's "The Machine Man of Ardathia" (*Amazing Stories,* November 1927), a time traveler from the future and a man in the present (the narrator) have the following exchange:

"I have just been five years into your future."

"My future!" I exclaimed. "How can that be when I have not lived it yet?"

"But of course you have lived it."

I stared, bewildered.

"Could I visit my past if you had not lived your future?"

CONSERVATION OF MASS-ENERGY IN TIME TRAVEL

The static concept of the block universe was invoked by one early science fiction fan who wrote in support of time travel, after another fan had cited a resulting failure of mass/energy conservation in time travel (in an attempt to debunk the possibility of time machines). This interesting exchange began with a Letter-to-the-Editor of *Astounding Stories* (November 1937), written in response to a time travel story the magazine had published a few months before:

> Let us say that there is, at a certain time, x amount of matter in the Universe, and e amount of energy. Then if a man of a mass travels backward in time to this particular instant aforementioned, the total amount of matter is thus $x + a$ while, if no other such mass-changing occurrences take place, the amount of matter in that future is $x - a$. Only a corresponding loss and gain respectively in the amount of energy could explain this conservation of energy and matter, advocates [of time travel] say what they may. But you can't rob or add energy to a Universe nilly-willy! Or perhaps time doesn't enter in on the matter. Perhaps you can add matter in a Universe provided you take it away on some future date.

This fan's concern may well have made an impression on science fiction writers, as one finds the necessity for conservation of energy explicitly stated in many of the time travel stories published afterwards, e.g., De Camp's classic 1941 novel *Lest Darkness Fall*. However, a rebuttal reply was received by the magazine in a letter (in the January 1938 issue) from another fan:

> [A recent letter] implies that the idea of time travel is incompatible with the law of conservation of mass and energy. I believe [the] reasoning is wrong [and that the] difficulty lies primarily in the assumption that a body moved in time is transported into a different Universe. According to Einstein, time and the three normal dimensions are so related as to form a continuous, inseparable medium we call the spacetime (sic) continuum. Time is in no way independent of the other components of our Universe. Hence a fixed mass [a time traveler and his machine] moved in time is by no means lost from the Universe, the action being

analogous to a shift along any other dimension.

The block universe of Minkowski is clearly reflected in those words, words remarkably modern in tone. Indeed, physicists have since discovered that the concept of energy conservation plays a far less central role in general relativity theory than it does in classical physics.

FREE WILL AND FATALISM

The block universe has important implications for theology, as well for physics, implications that go far beyond that of the words of the character in "Berkeley Square" quoted earlier in this chapter. In the *New Review* serialization of *The Time Machine*, for example, in a passage not appearing in the now-classic novella version of the story, the time traveler explains to his dinner guests:

> I'm sorry to drag in predestination and free will, but I'm afraid those ideas will have to help. . . . Suppose you knew fully the position and properties of every particle of matter, of everything existing in the Universe at any particular moment of time: suppose, that is, that you were omniscient. Well, that knowledge would involve the knowledge of the condition of things at the previous moment, and at the moment before that, and so on. If you knew and perceived the present perfectly, you would perceive therein the whole of the past. If you understood all natural laws the present would be a complete and vivid record of the past. Similarly, if you grasped the whole of the present, knew all its tendencies and laws, you would see clearly all the future. To an omniscient observer there would be no forgotten past—no piece of time as it were that had dropped out of existence—and no blank future of things yet to be revealed . . . present and past and future would be without meaning to such an observer. . . . He would see, as it were, a Rigid Universe filling space and time. . . . If "past" meant anything, it would mean looking in a certain direction, while 'future' meant looking the opposite way.

Wells's "Rigid Universe" certainly sounds like the block universe, and he seems to have believed that it held important implications for the concept of free will.

Before Minkowski, the debates over fatalism and free will had been in the exclusive province of philosophers, theologians and lawyers (if someone has no control over his actions, then how can we punish him if those actions constitute a crime?). After Minkowski and his block universe space-time, the physicists joined the debates. The major thrust behind such debates is, I think, the age-old dread that God's foreknowledge of our destiny can, in and of itself, impose that destiny upon us. The assumption here, of course, is that God is "outside of time" and so can take in the entire Minkowski block universe at a glance. Indeed, the relativistic view of the universe as a timeless, four-dimensional space-time seems to many to provide scientific, mathematical support for the conclusion that not only is the past fixed, but so is the future. Does this mean that the future is what it will be? (And if so, why bother agonizing over the many apparent decisions each of us faces every day?)

The block-universe, free-will issue has appeared in modern times in, of all places, the comics. One of Superman's more interesting adversaries in the 1950s was Mr. Mxyzptlk (pronounced *mix-yez-pittle-ick*), a being with seemingly magical powers who came from the Land of Zrfff in the fifth dimension. It isn't really magic, however, but "merely" space-time physics and geometry resulting from his one extra dimension. In one of his misadventures with Superman in 1954, Mr. Mxyzptlk begins selling the *Daily Mpftrz* in competition with the *Daily Planet*. Unlike the traditional newspaper that reports what has happened, the *Daily Mpftrz* prints what will happen. As Mr. Mxyzptlk explains, "You see, as a resident of the fifth dimension, I can get all the news I want from the *fourth* dimension!" The science editor at the *Daily Planet* explains the meaning of that to his boss, Perry White: "That's right, Mr. White . . . many physicists consider time the fourth dimension . . . so if Mr. Mxyzptlk can travel from the fifth dimension to our three-dimensional world, he most likely is able to see into the future!" Which leaves unanswered the question of why he continues to challenge Superman when he knows he will be defeated. (He always is.)

More traditional science fiction has also addressed the free-will issue. In W. Kubilius's "Turn Backward, O Time" (*Science Fiction Quarterly,* May 1951), a man in the twenty-fifth century is about to travel into the past to escape criminal prosecution. He is asked where he'd like to go, and he replies, "I do not understand the paradoxes—what if I choose to build gravity-deflectors in Ancient Rome?" When he is told (correctly, as I'll discuss in chapter eight) that such a thing can't happen because it didn't happen, he persists: "But if I can choose any period, it means that I can alter history at will—which presumes that the present can also be changed." At last, we get the explicit answer that bothers nearly everyone when they first hear it: "The real answer is that in the final analysis your decision to choose a certain time period is already made, and the things you will do [in the time traveler's proper time] are already determined. Free will is an illusion. It is synonymous with incomplete perception."

The rigidity of the future has received excellent treatment in science fiction as well. For example, in G. Eklund's "Stalking the Sun," we read of two time travelers from the past hunting men a half-million years in the future, for sport. When one of them wonders about the morality of killing a future man, he quickly rationalizes by saying, "This time, it isn't a real time. It's the future, but the future does not truly exist. To kill here is not real." His companion isn't so easily convinced, however, and he replies, "The timewarp was discovered twenty-five years ago. In that time, this time [the future] has not changed. My opinion is only my opinion. But I think this is it. The future. The only future. I think we're moving toward this no matter what we do. This is it."

For the purposes of time travel, it is of course mandatory to accept the reality of past and future, as is done in Harlan Ellison's story "Soldier." In that tale, originally published in 1957 and available today on videotape as an episode from *The Twilight Zone,* a soldier from the far future is hurled back to our time by the energy flux beam of enemy weapons' fire. The soldier tells stories of the utter horror of future warfare (and here Ellison unleashes a monstrous, graphic picture of horror in his description of telepathic "brain burners" and other terrors), and this generates a backlash to war. But even as peace engulfs the world, those remain who wonder if the future can be changed—perhaps it is rigidly frozen into a Minkowskian, Wellsian block universe. Perhaps today's peace movement, led by the soldier from tomorrow, is precisely what leads to the future at war. This is a theme that you, as a science fiction writer, can follow and keep consistent with modern physics.

And as for the persistence of the past, I find particularly romantic a passage from Grant Allen's introduction to his 1895 sleeping-into-the-future novel, *British Barbarians*:

> I am writing in my study on the heather-clad hilltop. When I raise my eye from my sheet of foolscap, it falls upon miles and miles of broad open moorland. My window looks out upon unsullied nature. Everything around is fresh and pure and wholesome. . . . But away below in the valley, as night draws on, a lurid glare reddens the north-eastern horizon. It marks the spot where the great wen of London heaves and festers.

It *is* tempting, don't you think, to imagine Allen is still there in his study in 1895, and to think heaving and festering late-Victorian London still there, too, with H.G. Wells himself in the middle of it, still reading the first rave reviews of *The Time Machine*.

SUMMARY

In this chapter the view of space-time as a four-dimensional hyperspace has been elaborated, and extended to include the concept of the *block universe*, a view of reality as rigid and unchangeable. The time travel implications of this view, concerning free will and the conservation of mass-energy, were explored in the words of both philosophers and science fiction writers.

CHAPTER 7

When General Relativity Made Time Travel to the Past Honest

I am especially intrigued by the spinning-Universe form of time travel, especially since . . . nobody has touched it. . . . But I should really stop mentioning the spinning-Universe in public, or somebody will nobble onto it before I can get into it!

from a 1970 letter by science fiction writer James Blish (quoted in David Ketterer's 1987 biography, *Imprisoned in a Tesseract*).

The eleventh-century Persian poet-philosopher Omar Khayyam was blunt in his evaluation of the likelihood of reliving the past; as he so beautifully wrote in one of the quatrains of the *Rubaiyat*:

> The Moving Finger writes; and, having writ,
> Moves on; nor all your Piety nor Wit

Shall lure it back to cancel half a Line,

Nor all your Tears wash out a Word of it.

And Wyn Wachhorst, a modern scholar of popular culture, has a curious, less poetic way of rejecting time travel in his essay on time travel in films. Transporting Wells's Victorian time traveler to the wrong century and invoking Einstein, he wrote in a scholarly essay, "We are indebted to H.G. Wells not only for the notion of voluntary time travel but also for the image by which we conceive it: a sunny, Edwardian [sic] gentleman perched on an ornate steam-age contraption that moves through time in much the same manner that a streetcar moves across town. This spatialized view of time, along with its Newtonian catechism, has increasingly gone the way of bowler hats and high button shoes in the new world of Einstein and quantum mechanics." The final sentence is particularly ironic because it is Einstein's field equations that actually provide the basis for the modern theory of time travel.

Well, you might say, these deniers of time travel are just story-tellers, philosophers, poets and magazine essayists—what do they know about the possibility of time travel? It is the thoughts of the physicists and mathematicians that are important because, if a time machine is ever built, it will be as a result of new understandings at a profoundly deeper level of mathematical physics than we have to-day. And curiously enough, there are physicists and mathematicians who think things may not be so gloomy concerning the possibilities of time travel. Kurt Gödel, one of the greatest mathematical logicians of all time, published (in 1949) a solution to Einstein's field equations for the case of a rotating universe that implies it is "theoretically possible in these worlds to travel into the past, or otherwise influence the past." That is, in Gödel's model of a universe there exist closed timelike world-lines in space-time. These world-lines are possible paths of space travelers, who always move into the local future but who nevertheless eventually arrive back in their own past. Such rotating-universe models had been studied as early as 1924, but it was Gödel who discovered their potential for backward time travel.

Gödel's hypothetical universe is infinite in extent, static (non-expanding) and rotating. Indeed, rotation is necessary in a static, infinite universe, as it keeps such a universe from collapsing under its own gravitational pull. It also has a nonzero cosmological constant (more on that in just a moment). The observable universe we live in is, however, expanding (as an astronomer would put it, our universe has an easily detected red shift), and its rotation rate is certainly less than one rotation every 70 billion years (which is too slow to result in closed timelike paths leading back into the past).

Besides the rotational issue, there is also a cosmological constant, a parameter in the field equations that Einstein included in 1917 precisely because he wanted a static, non-expanding universe to come out of general relativity. This requires that there be a long-range repulsive force to overcome the collapsing tendency of gravity. The cosmological constant must be nonzero, but all observational evidence indicates it is actually very nearly (if not exactly) zero. When Edwin Hubble discovered the universe is not static, but actually expanding, Einstein had to admit that his use of the cosmological constant was unnecessary and said it was probably the biggest mistake of his scientific life. With a zero cosmological constant, his equations predict the expansion of the universe, a prediction that would have been the crowning glory of general relativity.

In Gödel's time travel solution, the cosmological constant shows up in the expression for the radius of the minimum possible closed timelike curve; its square root appears in the denominator of this expression, and so if the constant is very small, the minimum radius is very big—in our universe the radius would be at least sixteen billion light years. So, while Gödel's theoretical solution satisfies the general relativity field equations, its time travel property does not hold in our universe.

(An aside: This conclusion would no doubt have greatly disappointed Gödel who, until he died in 1977, retained a keen interest in any observational data that might support the thesis that our universe is rotating. Despite his admitted concern over the possibility of a time traveler changing the past, or perhaps because of it, Gödel was utterly fascinated by the idea of time travel. It is now well-known that he was obsessed with his personal health and terrified at the thought of death. Speculation suggests that Gödel's interest in time travel was linked to an interest in the idea of reliving of one's life.)

It is an astonishing fact that one of the great twentieth-century physicists, Hermann Weyl (a colleague of both Einstein and Gödel at the Institute for Advanced Study in Princeton), wrote the following anticipatory passage three decades before Gödel (from his 1921 book *Space-Time-Matter*):

> It is possible to experience events now that will in part be an effect of my future resolves and actions. Moreover, it is not impossible for a world-line (in particular, that of my body), although it has a time-like direction at every point, to return to the neighborhood of a point which it has already once passed through. The result would be a spectral image of the world more fearful than anything the weird fantasy of E.T. Hoffmann [an early nineteenth-century German writer of the eccentric] has ever conjured up. In actual fact the very considerable fluctuations of the [components of the metric tensor, that describe how space-time 'curves'] that would be necessary to produce this effect do not occur in the region of the world in which we live . . . *Although paradoxes of this kind appear, nowhere do we find any real contradictions to the facts directly presented to us in experience* [my emphasis].

It would be thirty years after Weyl wrote these amazing words before Gödel presented his rotating-universe model showing how those "considerable fluctuations" might actually occur.

MEETING YOURSELF IN THE PAST

In the pivotal year of 1949, in an invited essay as part of his contribution to a study of Einstein's life work, Gödel specifically mentioned the paradoxical aspect of his time travel result:

> By making a round trip on a rocket ship in a sufficiently wide course, it is possible in these worlds to travel into any

region of the past, present, and future, and back again, exactly as it is possible in other worlds to travel to distant parts of space. This state of affairs *seems* [my emphasis] to imply an absurdity. For it enables one, e.g., to travel into the near past of those places where he has himself lived. There he would find a person who would be himself at some earlier period of his life. Now he could do something to this person which, by his memory, he knows has not happened to him.

It wouldn't be easy to actually fly a Gödelian rocket into the past. As Gödel showed, such a rocket would have to move at nearly 71 percent of the speed of light, and if the engines of the rocket ship were 100 percent efficient and could "transform matter completely into energy," the weight of the fuel would be greater than that of the rocket by a factor of 10^{22} divided by the square of the duration of the trip (in years, in rocket time). A trip to the past in Gödel's rotating universe, therefore, would require a time machine rocket looking something like Dr. Who's telephone booth attached to a fuel tank the size of several hundred trillion ocean liners!

Gödel defended his statements about the theoretical possibility of the paradoxes of a time traveler meeting himself in the past with what I think is an astonishingly unconvincing argument (and particularly so for a logician), an argument based primarily on the *engineering* limitations I just mentioned:

> This and similar contradictions, however, in order to prove the impossibility of the worlds under consideration, presuppose the actual feasibility of the journey into one's own past. But the velocities which would be necessary in order to complete the voyage in a reasonable time are far beyond everything that can be expected ever to become a practical possibility. Therefore it cannot be excluded *a priori*, on the ground of the argument given, that the space-time of the real world is of the type described.

With this odd argument, Gödel was trying to head off critics of his rotating-universe model, critics who might point to the time travel implication of the model as proof that the model is flawed. As I'll discuss in the next chapter, there is a far more satisfying way to answer Gödel's puzzle of changing the past, one that philosophers and physicists have only recently come to accept, but which some science fiction writers have used in their stories for decades.

An interesting assessment of the engineering difficulty was made by philosopher L. Sklar (and correctly so, in my opinion) a few years after Gödel's death. Concerning time travel in general (not just in Gödel's universe), and after first arguing for the logical possibility of closed timelike curves, Sklar wrote:

> There is, of course, the practical impossibility of traversing a closed timelike line. . . . While this does not constitute an in-principle rebuttal to the typical [grandfather paradox] objection to the possibility of closed timelike loops, it might be the ground for an argument to the following effect: "If there were such closed timelike loops, we would expect to observe many self-causing events. But we don't." Here the practical impossibility of traversing the loop is meant only to explain [that] the consequences of doing so wouldn't be commonly observed even if our world were causally pathological in this global sense. Plainly, as a refutation of the claim that closed causal loops are impossible since they *could* generate causal paradoxes, the mere invocation of practical impossibility of generating such a loop won't do.

EINSTEIN'S RESPONSE TO GÖDEL

Einstein wrote a reply to Gödel which seems to indicate the violation of causality that is inherent in time travel to the past had bothered Einstein from the beginning of his development of relativity:

> Kurt Gödel's essay constitutes, in my opinion, an important contribution to the general theory of relativity, especially to the analysis of the concept of time. The problem here involved disturbed me already at the time of the building up of the general

theory of relativity, without my having succeeded in clarifying it . . . the distinction "earlier-later" is abandoned for world-points which lie far apart in a cosmological sense, and those paradoxes, regarding the *direction* of the causal connection, arise, of which Mr. Gödel has spoken. . . . It will be interesting to weigh whether these are not to be excluded on physical grounds.

And, indeed, Gödel's analysis was later attacked (and also defended) on the basis of how to *physically* interpret his bizarre solution, not on whether he had made a mathematical error (today, after nearly a half-century of additional study, nobody has yet found such an error). And since 1949, other time travel solutions to the field equations have been found, solutions that have nothing to do with a rotating universe, so time travel is no mere anomaly of Gödel's particular analysis. Rather, time travel is literally built into the gravitational field equations, independent of how the actual universe may actually be, rotating or not.

Gödel's idea of meeting yourself in the past has a long literary history that greatly predates both Gödel and science fiction. You can find a brief description of *almost* such an encounter, for example, in Goethe's autobiography from more than a century and a half ago. (*Almost*, because the experience of the young Goethe and the memory of the older Goethe eight years later are, like Gödel's example, not quite the same.) And in Osbert Sitwell's 1929 travelogue disguised as a novel, *The Man Who Lost Himself*, the author used 280 pages to get to his then-shocking conclusion—a man is apparently killed by his younger self.

Science fiction has, of course, had a simply wonderful time with self-encounters, mostly in the bizarre situation called a *causal loop*, something I'll discuss in great detail in the next chapter. But just to whet your appetite, let me give you three story examples of near self-encounters to show how dramatic this situation can be. In Jack Williamson's "Minus Sign" (*Astounding Science Fiction*, November 1942), a spaceship fights a battle with itself as it self-interacts while traveling backward in time. In Frederik Pohl's "Let the Ants Try," a time traveler journeys back forty million years. Upon stepping out of his time machine, he hears a "raucous animal cry" from somewhere in the nearby jungle. Later, after other adventures in time, he returns to near the same point in space-time. Indeed, after stepping out of his time machine he sees himself in the distance—the version of himself during his first trip. Then, suddenly, the time traveler meets a violent death: "As his panicky lungs filled with air for the last time, he knew what animal had screamed in the depths of the Coal Measure forest." And in D. Bilenkin's short story "The Uncertainty Principle," a time traveler happens across his own grave while on a visit to the Middle Ages. Hence he learns, in a rather awful way, that he will die during a future trip through time even further back into the past.

Hollywood, too, has had fun with self-encounters. The original 1985 *Back to the Future* film has a wonderful near-miss in it; at the end Marty McFly returns to the future (his present) ten minutes before he left for the past (at the start of the movie), and so at the end he is able to watch himself leave at the beginning. The filmmakers were so fascinated by this idea that in their 1989 sequel *Back to the Future II* they wrote self-meetings for four different characters. Self-encounters also occur in the far less charming 1994 film *Timecop*. (This film is "good" for aspiring time travel writers to see how many logical bloopers you can spot—there are many.)

SUMMARY

This chapter continued the discussion of the theoretical justification for time travel to the past which we began in chapter three; Einstein's theory of curved space-time as an explanation for gravity (the general theory of relativity). I explained how Einstein's friend, mathematician Kurt Gödel, found the first backward-in-time solutions to the gravitational field equations in 1949. Gödel also showed how to "fly into the past" with a rocketship. While Gödel had some difficulties understanding all the implications, he was fascinated by the paradox of a time traveler meeting himself in the past. I included examples of such meetings, from both written stories and films.

CHAPTER 8

Paradoxes

Changing the Past,
Causal Loops and Sex

He felt the intellectual desperation of any honest philosopher. He knew that he had about as much chance of understanding such problems as a collie has of understanding how dog food gets into cans.

> a time traveler, perplexed by paradoxes in Robert
> Heinlein's classic tale "By His Bootstraps."

What was this time traveling? A man couldn't cover himself with dust by rolling in a paradox, could he?

> the incredulous Editor, astonished at the disheveled
> appearance of Wells's time traveler upon his return
> from A.D. 802,701 and beyond.

Not too many years ago the philosopher Q. Smith, who believes in the finite length of the past, wrote an analysis to refute the logical arguments presented by the eighteenth-century philosopher Immanuel Kant for his belief in an infinite past. Although the paper had nothing to do with paradoxes of time travel to the past, Smith wrote this passage in the course of presenting his case:

> Why does the sun arise in the morning and not at some
> other time? Why do the hands of a properly functioning clock

point to 12:00 at noon and midnight and not at other times?
Why does the death of a person occur at a later time than his
birth? The answer in all these cases is: Because by the very
nature of these events they could not occur at other times. It
belongs to the very nature of the sun's rising that it occur in
the morning and not in the afternoon or evening. It belongs
to the very nature of the hands of a properly functioning clock
to point at 12:00 at noon and midnight and not at other times.
And it belongs to the very nature of birth to occur at a time
earlier than a person's death.

You might or might not laugh at this (laughter is a tempting
reaction because it seems to be a big deal over semantics—right?),
but perhaps there is more to it. Indeed, there is more to it than even
Smith saw. For example, what would he say about a time traveler
born in 1940 who enters a time machine in 1999, pushes a few
buttons, and then boldly steps out into the Cretaceous period seventy million years earlier and is eaten for lunch by a passing Tyran-
nosaurus rex? Perhaps Smith would say that there is no contradiction between this situation and his third claim because in the time
traveler's proper time, her death follows her birth. However, many
would consider a woman dying before her parents are born a paradox, plain and simple, say what you will about proper time.

Time travel is, of course, full of paradoxes. A paradox, according
to the usual dictionary definition, is something that appears to contain contradictory or incompatible parts, seemingly reducing the
whole to nonsense. Yet, there is also evident truth to the whole.
That's the paradox. The history of science and mathematics has left
a long trail of paradoxes, with those associated with time travel
merely among the most recent. Not all the puzzles of time travel
involve physics. For example, philosopher L. Dwyer has observed:

Doubtless time travel will raise a host of legal difficulties,
e.g., should the time traveler who punches his younger self
(or vice versa) be charged with assault? Should the time traveler who murders someone and then flees to the past for sanc-

tuary be tried in the past for his crime committed in the future? If he marries in the past can he be tried for bigamy even though his other wife will not be born for almost 5000 years? Etc., etc. I leave such questions for lawyers and writers of ethics textbooks to solve.

Interestingly, since Dwyer wrote this passage, the ethical issues raised by time travel have become a significant point of discussion in popular entertainment. Television's *Quantum Leap*, for example, based essentially all four years of its episodes on the ethics of tampering with the past.

Consider the following exchange between the inventor of a time machine and his helper in F. Flagg and W. Wright's "Time Twister" (*Thrilling Wonder Stories*, October 1947); note the hint of sexual paradox winked at in the original *Back to the Future* film:

"You mean to say," he questioned incredulously, "that I could go back a hundred years?"

"If you had the proper machine in which to travel, yes."

"But that'd take me back to before I was born."

The Professor smiled tolerantly.

"Look at this diagram, Hank. This line is the time continuum. It incorporates space, too. This dot is you. It doesn't matter when you were born, or when you will die. You exist right now, that's the fact. Traveling into the past or future wouldn't make you grow any younger or older. Such a thought is naive. Let me demonstrate the mechanics of it for you. If . . . we calculate with non-Euclidean mathematics. . . ."

"It don't sound reasonable," the farmhand objected. "If I went back—"

"I know," interjected the Professor, "if you went back you might meet your own father as a young man and you'd be older than he, or maybe he and your mother would be kids going to school."

"Haw, haw! That'd be funny, that would."

One way science fiction writers respond to the puzzles of time travel is to give up and to concede that the logical paradoxes are overwhelming. This is the position of the history graduate student in M.J. Costello's 1990 novel *Time of the Fox*, for example; when he learns that the Columbia University physics department is doing experiments in time travel, he blurts out, "I'm no physicist, but even I know the logical difficulties with time travel. It's open season on coherent history, with goofy paradoxes. . . . Lots of fun for stories but absolutely crackers as a real possibility."

H.G. Wells's failure to use paradox in *The Time Machine* surprises most readers when they first encounter the work, and one of the first reviews took him to task on that very point. Wells, it should go without saying, was a brilliant intellect and was not oblivious to the possibility of paradoxes in time travel, but his failure to use them seems to indicate that he simply did not know how to respond to such puzzles. In the opening of the novella during the dinner party at which the time traveler tries to convince his friends of the possibility of a time machine, one of them observes, "It would be remarkably convenient for the historian. One might travel back and verify the accepted account of the Battle of Hastings, for instance." To this another guest replies, "Don't you think you would attract attention? Our ancestors had no great tolerance for anachronisms." The time traveler has no reply to any of this because, I believe, Wells had no reply.

Paradoxes offend common sense. They can irritate, too. The specialists who study time travel paradoxes in Barry Malzberg's 1978 novel *Chorale* make their colleagues in the Department of Reconstruction (of the past) uncomfortable with their constant worrying about altering history: "The paradoxologists were a stuffy bunch, and no one liked them very much." But are there really paradoxes at all? As the time traveler in F.J. Bridge's "Via the Time Accelerator" (*Amazing Stories*, January 1931) coolly declares to a friend after an astonishing adventure in the year A.D. 1,001,930: "Paradoxical? My dear fellow, the Einstein Theory is full of apparent paradoxes, yet to him who understands it there is no inconsistency whatever. Give me another cigarette, will you, Frank?" Somewhat more concerned about time travel paradoxes, however, is the time traveler in Eando Binder's "The Time Cheaters" (*Thrilling Wonder Stories*, March 1940), who tells his partner just before their first trip into the future: "I'm not sure any more about getting back. There're some unpredictable terms in the time-travel equation—paradoxes. Maybe we won't get back."

The fear of time travelers from the future attempting to alter the past has led some philosophers and physicists to assert that time travel is impossible because it would imply that the impossible could happen, i.e., changing the past. This concern is described in Tim Powers's 1983 novel *The Anubis Gates*. When one of the time travelers in that work finds himself stranded in London of 1810, he takes solace with the thought, "I could invent things—the light bulb, the internal combustion engine, . . . flush toilets. . . ." But then he thinks better of doing any of those things: "No, better not to do anything to change the course of recorded history—any such tampering might cancel the trip I got here by, or even the circumstances under which my mother and father met. I'll have to be careful. . . ."

Contrary to this character's thinking is the modern view of what time travel to the past would actually mean. The modern view is that you could not travel anywhere/when into the past unless you've already been there, and when you do make the trip you will do exactly what you've already done there. You could not tamper with the past in the way described in J.B. Ryan's "The Mosaic" (*Astounding Science Fiction*, July 1940). In that story, the Moslem defeat by Christians in A.D. 732 is originally a Moslem victory. Centuries later the first time traveler (a Moslem) accidently changes the victory into a defeat, and he vanishes at the crucial instant "with all the suddenness of a bursting bubble. And with him into nothingness, across the gulf of Time" went all the history after A.D. 732, changed to our world's history that records the ancient victory of Cross over Crescent. The modern view considers this nonsense.

This does not mean a time traveler will necessarily be ineffectual during a stay in the past. Not being able to change the past is not equivalent to being unable to influence or affect the past. You cannot

prevent either the Black Death in 1665 London or the Great Fire
the following year, but it is logically possible that you—a careless
time traveler—could be the cause of either or both. In my own story
"Newton's Gift," (*Omni*, January 1979), it is the gift of a time traveler
from the future (an electronic calculator) that causes Newton's de-
scent from first-rate physics to third-rate theology (Newton thinks
such an incredible gadget can only be the work of the Devil); the
time traveler knew of Newton's change of focus from historical records (but he didn't know the reason for it).

The distinction between changing and affecting the past has been
understood only in relatively recent times. Recall from the previous
chapter that even the great Gödel slipped on this point when he
wrote of a time traveler being able to visit himself in the past (that's
OK) and then doing something he does not remember having done
(that's not OK). To illustrate Gödel's view from a different angle,
consider G. Hunter's story "Journey" (*Fantasy and Science Fiction*,
February 1951) in which we find a thirteen-year-old boy in Southern
California going forward in time from 1935 to 1950 to meet himself.
It happens on a day he plays hookey, taking a streetcar into Los
Angeles—suddenly he finds himself in the future with no explanation (making this more fantasy than science fiction, but that's OK
for us, here). After seeing a movie, he locates his adult-self and
discovers he will be (is) unhappily married, with all his ambitions
unfulfilled.

It is then that the Gödelian objection occurs to him (remember
this story was written in 1951 just two years after Gödel wrote his
paper), and so he asks his older-self, "Wouldn't *you* remember [all
this] happening to you when [*you*] were thirteen?" The answer
comes back (one Gödel himself apparently never thought of): "One
time when I was your age I can remember ditching school and
hopping a streetcar to L.A. I know I went to a movie." But, the adult
self couldn't remember what had happened after the movie. In an
attempt to change his life, the adult self puts his younger self on a
streetcar back home (and to his past) with the admonition, "Damn
you, *don't forget!*" And the happy (and illogical) ending is that he

doesn't forget—and so presumably the future is changed. Isaac Asimov tripped over the mirror image of this error—and he didn't often trip—when he wrote (in "Time Travel," *Asimov's Science Fiction Magazine*, April 1984) that "to go into the past and do *anything* would change a great deal of what followed, perhaps everything that followed." Not true.

The idea that the past might be changed and then consciously changed back again if things don't improve can be found in a number of different literary forms. The earliest example I know is the 1937 stage play by Maxwell Anderson, *The Star-Wagon*. There a proverbial self-taught inventor, when told by his wife of thirty-five years that perhaps their marriage has been a mistake, travels back to 1902 to give them both a chance to make a new future. When once again we see them in 1937, matters are much worse with their new mates. So, back again goes the time traveler to 1902 to put things back the way they were.

Mixing "changing-the-past" with irony (always an entertaining mix, if you can pull it off) is the presentation in J.W. Farrell's "All Our Yesterdays" (*Super Science Stories*, April 1949), a tale of the far future, when watching the past on a TV-like screen is a pastime of the elite upper classes. One of these idlers shows his girlfriend the execution of a criminal a thousand years in the past (in 1949, of course), and then the commission of the actual crime which demonstrates that the condemned man was really innocent. She pleads with him to change the past. He at first resists, saying:

> My dear girl, don't be absurd! To alter the objective past would be like kicking out the bottom block of a tower. We are built on the past . . . If [the criminal lived, some of his] descendants would be alive today. And who knows what alterations they would have made?

She persists, however, and he finally yields—with disastrous results. With the past changed, the watcher is no longer a privileged upper-class social parasite, but he is now a beggar on Mars panhandling for the rocket fare back to Earth.

A common logical error in change-the-past tales is nicely illustrated in the opening scenes of the 1989 movie *Time Trackers*.
There, a laboratory coffee cup is broken just before the first time
machine trip into the past. The laboratory staff realizes the experiment is a success even before the traveler returns, when the cup is
no longer broken—the time traveler caught it before it hit the floor.
So the past has been changed, but the broken cup is still remem-
bered, even though it now never happened. Change-the-past stories
can be fun, sure, but don't make this particularly elementary error
in your tales.

To understand why I reject the logic of changing-the-past tales
(while admitting that I can still personally enjoy them), consider
C.L. Moore's classic 1936 story "Tryst in Time," where we find the
following dialogue between two characters discussing the possible
damage that might result if a time traveler should somehow change
his own past:

> "Suppose you landed in your own past?" queried Eric.
> Dow smiled.
> "The eternal question," he said. "The inevitable objection
> to the very idea of time travel. Well, you never did, did you?
> You know it never happened!"

THE GRANDFATHER PARADOX

The classic change-the-past paradox is the so-called grandfather paradox, which poses the question: What happens if an assassin goes
back in time and murders his grandfather before his (the assassin's)
own father is conceived? If his father is never born, neither is the
assassin, and so how can he go back to murder his grandfather?
When all is said about the impossibility of changing the past, most
people still wonder why the time traveler can't kill his grandfather.
There the time traveler is, after all, just two feet away from the nasty
young codger (I assume he is nasty to make the unpleasant business
of murder as palatable as possible), with a perfectly functioning,
well-oiled revolver in his hand, cocked and loaded with powerful

factory-fresh ammunition that even Dirty Harry would find excessive. What can possibly prevent the time traveler from simply raising his arm and doing the deed?

The opening illustration to Mort Weisinger's "Thompson's Time Traveling Theory" (*Amazing Stories*, March 1944) shows this act in detail, including the smoking gun in the hand of the time traveler who has just taken a shot at grandpop. And if that still leaves open the remote possibility of an aiming error through nervousness, why can't a suicidal time traveler wrap his entire body in factory-fresh dynamite and blow up granddad (as well as himself and everything else within a hundred feet)?

One amusing story (P.S. Miller's "Status Quondam") pushes the grandfather paradox to its logical limit to illustrate the risks a time traveler takes by indulging in combat in the past. Having traveled to Greece in the fifth century B.C., this tale's protagonist suddenly realizes (with just a little exaggeration): "Ninety-five generations back you'd have more grandfathers than there are people on Earth, or stars in the Galaxy! You're kin to everyone. . . . You as much as take a poke at anyone, and the odds are you won't even get to be a twinkle in your daddy's eye."

One science fiction solution to the "killing your ancestors or your younger-self" paradoxes (one that Moore used in "Tryst in Time") is the ultimate failure of the murder; e.g., the gun jams, the knife blade snaps, a wind gust blows the poison dart off target, the murderer faints just before he can do the foul deed, etc. No matter how many times the murderer tries, and no matter how clever his scheme, he fails. Physicist/philosopher David Malament of the University of Chicago forcefully rebutted the illogic of arguing-by-paradox when he wrote:

> [One] view is that time-travel . . . is simply absurd and leads to logical contradictions. You know how the argument goes. If time travel were possible, one could go backward in time and undo the past. One could bring it about that both conditions P and *not-P* obtain at some point in space-time. For example, I

could go back and kill my earlier infant self making it impossible for my earlier self to ever grow up to be me. *I simply want to remark that arguments of this type have never seemed convincing to me . . . The problem with these arguments is that they simply do not establish what they are supposed to* [my emphasis]. To be sure, if I could go back and kill my infant self, some sort of contradiction would arise. But the only conclusion to draw from this is that if I tried to go back and kill my infant self then, for some reason, I would fail. Perhaps I would trip at the last minute. The usual arguments do not establish that time travel is impossible, but only that if it *were* possible, certain actions could not be performed.

This particular approach to addressing time travel paradoxes (with which I happen to agree) is of particular interest to theologians because it is directly related to the question of free will versus fatalism. That is, are humans the creators of the future, or are they mere fated puppets of destiny? Is a time traveler to the past unable to alter events because that was the *only* way they could happen? Such questions are, of course, precisely what has attracted philosophers and theologians to time travel. If a time traveler can visit the past and is able to change events, then paradoxes like the grandfather one could result. But if a time traveler cannot change events, then *why* not? Is free will simply an illusion? And what if we could visit the future and return to the present—could we change the future?

Interesting variations on physical backward time travel in science fiction, which neatly avoid the paradoxes of interacting with and changing the past, use gadgets that let story characters simply hear or see the remote past (as in "All Our Yesterdays," but without the ability to make changes). A tool designed for this purpose is the "time viewer" in D. Franson's "One Time in Alexandria" (*Analog*, June 1980), which allows its archaeologist-user to learn the horrifying answer to how the ancient Library at Alexandria was really burned to the ground.

A second fictional way to squirm out of the change-the-past/free will problem was conceived by the well-known electrical engineer and science fiction writer, John R. Pierce. In his "Mr. Kinkaid's Pasts," we read "There is no unique past! The uncertainty principle of Heisenberg, which philosophers use to assure us that the world is not a predestined machine, without room for free will, leading to one unique future, just as decisively contradicts the idea of a unique past . . . there is an infinity of pasts which are consistent with all the evidences in our present Universe, and any of these pasts is as much the real past as any other." In other words, the state of the world now neither determines the state tomorrow with certainty, nor was the state today determined with certainty by the state yesterday. Thus, no paradox can result from tampering with the past since the state of the past does not matter anyway (This seemingly bizarre idea has since found comfort in the so-called "many-worlds interpretation" of quantum mechanics, discussed in more length in chapter eleven.)

All of the above examples simply avoid the real issue. We are interested in the paradoxes of time travel because the physics says it really can be done. One recent science fiction novel takes the position that nature will subtly avoid paradoxes, automatically. In the 1994 *Dead Morn* (by Piers Anthony and Roberto Fuentes), a time traveler from 2413 visits the revolutionary Cuba of the late 1950s and early 1960s in an attempt to change history (and thus patch-up his own rather dismal times). While in the past, he not only discovers the presence of a "paradox shield" that prevents him from acts such as killing his own ancestors, but also that "the shield had to act in a natural or coincidental fashion, lest it create paradox itself by overt manifestations." Such a shield puts a crimp on the time traveler's actions, of course, but not for long because when you write non-scientific science fiction you can make your own rules (remember my comments on this in the introduction?) And so the authors have their time traveler overwhelm the shield by embarrassing it: "He could fight the shield by forcing it to be obvious." Apparently, according to this line of reasoning, when caught with its fingers in the cookie jar, physics simply blushes and withdraws its objections. In my humble opinion, dear reader, this is hard to swallow.

L. Sprague de Camp's earlier, famous story "A Gun for Dinosaur" has a different view that puts forth the terrifying idea that nature itself will take any corrective action necessary to avoid paradoxes, but subtlety is not required. The story has two big-game hunter-guides using a time machine to operate a safari-for-hire business, taking hunters back to the late Mesozoic era. When a disgruntled client tries to go back in time (to shoot the guides, who had, or rather would displease him the following day), we learn just how nasty de Camp thinks Mother Nature might be in order to prevent a paradox (the guides had not been shot on the original safari, so they could not be shot):

> The instant James started [to ambush the guides] the space-time forces snapped him forward to the present to prevent a paradox. And the violence of the passage practically tore him to bits [making his body look] as if every bone in it had been pulverized and every blood vessel burst, so it was hardly more than a slimy mass of pink protoplasm.

As the rest of this chapter will demonstrate, killing your grandfather (or any other ancestor) is logically impossible—forget the physics. No one will ever find a note in the empty laboratory of a missing time traveler who, skeptical of the grandfather paradox, has written: "To prove the falsity of the grandfather paradox, I will take my time machine back fifty years and kill my grandf—" Nor will the inventor of a time machine need be concerned about the pretty little twist in Fredric Brown's "First Time Machine," in which the inventor of a time machine shows the gadget to three friends. One of the friends then steals the machine to kill his grandfather sixty years in the past; the story closes with a repeat of the opening, with the inventor showing the gadget to two friends.

It is a shame that the classic time travel paradox takes such a murderous form, but that is the historical origin of the idea. One Letter-to-the-Editor of *Astounding Stories* (January 1933) commented as follows: "Why pick on grandfather? It seems that the only way to prove that time travel is impossible is to cite a case of killing one's own grandfather. This incessant murdering of harmless ancestors must stop. Let's see some wide-awake fan make up some other method of disproving the theory." As we proceed in this book, you'll see the wit of those who have answered that fan's plea; but even today, as it stands revealed as a red herring, it is the grandfather paradox that stands preeminent. As one of the characters in "Thompson's Time Travel Theory" (a tale that does get the grandfather paradox right) concludes, incorrectly, the grandfather paradox "proves" that "all time traveling stories are one hundred percent sheer oil of over ripe bananas!"

The philosopher S. Gorovitz has written, concerning time travel and its concomitant backward causation (c.g., the apparent possibility of a time traveler killing his grandfather), that the subject gives "rise to such puzzles that we are forced to question its intelligibility." Gorovitz correctly believes that the past cannot be changed, and so this act of violence simply can't happen. He goes on to say that the inability of the time traveler to kill his grandfather faces us with the problem of explaining why the time traveler cannot fire the gun or, if he can, why he can only fire in specific directions. Gorovitz asserts that there can be only two possible answers: "Either the gun is not behaving as the normal physical object we take it to be, or the notion of voluntary action does not apply in the usual way." Here, at last, we have explicit concern over the issue of free will and time travel. (Notice, however, that the time traveler could kill himself in the past without paradox.)

Gorovitz has gotten himself into his logical quagmire precisely because he is thinking of the past as happening twice—once without the time traveler and his gun, and again with him and his gun. With this second chance, Gorovitz argues, the time traveler should have the ability to do something that wasn't done on the first pass through history. So why can't he? The puzzle is all Gorovitz's own making because he is violating his own fundamental belief in the unchangeable nature of the past. Assuming that the time traveler did once confront his grandfather, then he must fail because he did fail. To demand an accounting for the specific why of the failure before accepting the failure is a misguided yet common mistake. (His refusal to accept this failure is like a stranded motorist refusing to believe his car won't start until he knows why.)

THE TIME POLICE

Over the years a lot of science fiction writers have either missed the previous point or have chosen to ignore it. In their stories we find forces (mysterious and otherwise) devised to protect the fragile past from future tampering, e.g., the so-called "time police." These temporal commandos roam the corridors of time, disrupting the plans of those who would change history to suit their personal desires. Such people do not necessarily have to be evil and, indeed, science fiction writers have been quite inventive about possible altruistic motives for a desire to change the past. For example, in John Brunner's "Host Age," operatives of the Corps of Temporal Adjustment (from the year 2620) intentionally change the past by infecting the present with a terrible disease for which there is no defense. The reason for this seemingly irrational (and, I might add, illogical) act is clever in its simplicity: Over the centuries medicine has triumphed over all known ills, and so when alien invaders infect humankind with a new and vicious plague, there are no natural defenses. So, back in time go the Corps to alter history so humans will have developed natural antibodies before the invasion occurs in the far future. But not a word about the grandfather paradox, which literally demands some attention.

Still, while often entertaining, such tales are really just westerns, mysteries, police procedurals, or some other similar specialty story form, wearing thin camouflage. Such a story device can be, as the philosopher D. Lewis put it, "a boring invasion." So why do we find it so often in fiction, as in the forms of the Time Security Commission in Chad Oliver's 1955 "A Star Above It" (which prevents a rogue historian from changing the past to allow the Aztecs to defeat Cortez) and the operatives in Poul Anderson's many stories about the time patrol? We often see the concept in the movies, too, e.g., the time-police films *Trancers* (1985) and *Timecop*. These plots are prevalent because the writers feel, as do many philosophers (and even some physicists, who should know better), it is the only way to have both time travel and free will.

In an attempt to analyze the free-will issue in time travel in the context of the grandfather paradox, the philosopher Γ. Thom presents an interesting grammatical argument. Professor Thom asks us to imagine the usual situation: a time traveler as a mature man travels into the past and confronts himself as a boy. Can the time traveler kill the boy (himself)? Thom argues the answer is yes, but also that he won't because he didn't. The fact that he won't (didn't) doesn't mean he can't (couldn't). Thom pursues this further and says that if the time traveler can, then one would appear safe in assuming that there is no logical inconsistency in imagining this "could happen" event actually occurring. But, of course, the time traveler killing his younger version would lead to a logical paradox, thus seeming to refute the possibility of a possible event actually occurring. If this is the case, what does *possible* mean?

Philosopher J. Meiland has given a nice answer to Thom's puzzle. He writes of time travel suicide:

> If we assume that it is impossible for [a time traveler] to kill his younger self, some people are inclined to ask such questions as this: "But how can the laws of logic prevent him from killing his younger self? Do they cause his finger to slip on the trigger or the bullet to fly apart in mid-air?" The implication of such questions is that laws of logic cannot prevent such actions. But such questions are like asking: "How do the laws of logic prevent the geometer from trisecting the angle or squaring the circle? Do they, for example, cause his ruler to slip at a crucial moment every time he tries it?"

The answer is, of course, no. Trisecting an angle and squaring the circle (with just a straight-edge and compass) are *logically* impossible, and free will is simply irrelevant. The same is true with time travel to the past and changing the past.

The correct view of such matters can be found in Robert Heinlein's 1964 novel *Farnham's Freehold*, the story of a family that is literally blasted twenty-one centuries into the future when their bomb shelter receives a direct hit from a Soviet nuclear warhead in World War III. There we find the following exchange between two characters who are about to return to their original time via a time machine:

> "The way I see it, there are no paradoxes in time travel, there can't be. If we are going to make this time jump, then we already did; that's what happened. And if it doesn't work, then it's because it didn't happen."
>
> "But it hasn't happened yet. Therefore, you are saying that it didn't happen, so it can't happen. That's what I said."
>
> "No, no! We don't know whether it has already happened or not. If it did, it will. If it didn't, it won't."

PRINCIPLE OF SELF-CONSISTENCY

Modern philosophers, and many physicists as well, who have examined the concept of time travel agree with this explanation from Heinlein's character, and they now use the so-called *principle of self-consistency*. The principle simply says that the only solutions to the laws of physics are those that are globally self-consistent. That is, paradoxes can't happen. An intuitive understanding of the principle (which physicists have recently *derived* as a consequence of other, more traditional principles in physics) can be found in mainstream literature from long ago. For example, in Lord Dunsany's short 1928 play *The Jest of Hahalaba*, a man obtains (via supernatural means) a copy of tomorrow's newspaper. In it he reads his own obituary, which so shocks him he promptly expires—thus explaining the obituary.

Despite the principle of self-consistency, which renders the grandfather paradox moot, there is a different class of paradox that is mysterious to this day. It has been nicely illustrated by the philosopher L. Dwyer in a little story of a time traveler who journeys back to 3000 B.C.: "In our time travel story it just may be that the traveler's interest in going back to ancient Egypt is stimulated by recently discovered documents, found near Cairo, containing the diary of a person claiming to be a time traveler; whereupon our hero, realizing it is himself, immediately begins . . . construction of a rocket in order to 'fulfill his destiny.' " In other words, (a) he builds a Gödelian rocket and goes back to the past because of the discovered diary, and (b) the diary is discovered because he goes back to the past. Both (a) and (b) alone have logical clarity, but together they form a closed time loop of enormous mystery.

The general plot device of a closed time loop artifact has a long tradition in science fiction. In the early story by F. Bridge, "Via the Time Accelerator" (*Amazing Stories*, January 1931), for example, we find one of the first sophisticated treatments of causal loops in the genre. A time traveler in 1930, about to start his journey into the future in an airplane/time machine, wonders at the last moment if he should really go--and then he sees himself returning and thus knows he will successfully make the trip. As he later tells a friend:

> That decided me . . . Paradoxical? I should say so! I had seen myself return from my time trip before I had started it; had I not seen that return, I would not have commenced that strange journey, and so could not have returned in order to induce me to decide that I would make the journey!

And later, when he finds himself in a dangerous situation in the future, he draws hope from the earlier experience:

> I would escape. . . . It was so decreed. Had I not, with my own eyes, seen myself appear out of the fourth dimension back there in the Twentieth Century, and glide down to my landing-field? Surely, then, I *was* destined to return to my own age safe and sound.

Even more dramatic is the second, internal loop that ends the story. When the time traveler arrives in a ruined city in the year A.D. 1,001,930, he is greeted, by name, by an old man who says he is the Last Man alive. The Last Man knew the time traveler was coming because an ancient history book had said the Last Man had, in fact, appeared from the future in A.D. 502,101 in the very time machine out of which the time traveler had just stepped. The time traveler is so startled by this bizarre story that he decides to mull it over until the next day. As he wakes up in the morning, he is just in time to see the Last Man stealing the time machine to depart for 502,101. Stranded in the future, the time traveler wanders the city in despair until he chances upon a museum. And there, sealed in a glass case, is his time machine! It has been there for half a million years, since the end of the Last Man's journey. And so the time traveler is saved; he merely adds some oil to the still functional engine (if you can accept time travel, I suppose this is no more difficult to believe) and returns to 1930—just as he saw himself do at the start of this imaginative tale.

SEXUAL PARADOXES

There is no question about it—to say causal loops are counter-intuitive is to barely hint at their mystery; but they are not an argument against time travel. Rather, if time travel is possible, then it would seem we have to accept causal loops, too. Let me conclude this chapter by pointing out to you that there are causal loops even stranger than the ones already discussed, hard as that may be to believe. These are the sexual paradoxes (as a character in Silverberg's 1969 novel *Up the Line* declares with interesting enthusiasm, "You haven't lived until you've laid one of your own ancestors").

Philosophers have found sexual time travel paradoxes full of dramatic appeal. For example, as a challenge problem to the readers of the journal *Analysis*, British philosopher J. Harrison posed the following astonishing situation: A young lady, one Jocasta Jones, one day finds an ancient deep freezer containing a solidly frozen young man. She thaws him out and learns that his name is Dum and that he possesses a book that describes how to make both a deep freezer and a time machine. They marry. Soon they have a baby boy and name him Dee. Years later, after reading his father's book, Dee makes a time machine. Dee and Dum, taking the book with them, get into the machine and begin a trip into the past. Running out of food during the lengthy journey, Dee kills his father and eats him. Arriving at last in the past, Dee dismantles the time machine and uses the parts to make a deep freezer (again, using the book's instructions), gets into it, and . . . wakes up to find a young lady, one Jocasta Jones, has thawed him out. When asked his name, he replies Dum, shows Jocasta his book, they marry, and. . . .

Professor Harrison concluded this amazing tale with a challenge question for his readers: "Did Jocasta commit a logically possible crime?" This issue is just the bare surface of an ocean of puzzles. Jocasta's crime, of course, is that she has seemingly (if unwittingly) committed incest; readers who remember their Greek mythology and the story of Oedipus and his mother/wife will now see why Harrison named his heroine as he did. But what of Dee's crime? He has, after all, eaten his father. But perhaps it isn't a crime because of course Dee and Dum are one-in-the-same, and is it a crime to eat yourself? According to one of Harrison's professional colleagues, M. MacBeath, this tale is "a story so extravagant in its implications that it will be regarded by many as an effective *reductio ad absurdum* of the one dubious assumption on which the story rests: the possibility of time travel."

Harrison's challenge provoked nearly a dozen replies. Not one mentioned what I consider the real puzzle in the tale—who wrote that interesting little book on how to make a time machine, and when? The most thoughtful response received did make the interesting observation that not only has Jocasta committed incest, but she has done so with a single act of intercourse. It is important to understand that, in a block universe, the events in a causal loop do not happen endlessly, but only once. Jocasta thaws Dum (Dee) out just once, marries him just once, and the two consummate their marriage just once (or at least conceive their child just once). Ordinarily we think it takes two sexual acts to commit incest, the first resulting in the birth of a child, the second being union with the child, but it is not so in this causal loop.

And finally, in another response to the challenge, one reader made the telling point that irrespective of physics, the story of

Jocasta is biologically flawed, and fatally so. As he wrote: "The bio-logical problem is the following. Dee is the son of Dum and Jocasta. So Dee obtained half his genes from Dum and half from Jocasta. But Dum is diachronically identical with Dee, and is therefore geno-typically identical to him (i.e., himself). That is, Dee is both genotypi-cally identical and distinct from Dum, which is absurd." Amazingly, Professor Harrison's reply was to not be perturbed at all, dismissing it as a mere "law of nature, not of logic." But if one is going to ignore laws of nature, why bother debating time travel (or anything) in physics? Conservation of momentum is not a law of logic either; should we overlook it when it suits us as well? I don't think so.

In spite of the biological flaw, the sexual loops-in-time story has proven to be enormously popular, and probably will continue to be. Forget the physics, people are always going to be interested in sex! But it is getting harder all the time to write stories that are even as good as the classics of the past. I discuss several of those tales in *Time Machines*, but the one you certainly want to read is Heinlein's 1959 "All You Zombies—," generally thought to be the best sexual paradox, causal loop story ever written. Indeed, in a 1958 letter to his literary agent, Heinlein wrote, "I hope that I have written in that story the Farthest South in time paradoxes." In my humble opinion, he did, and you should read it to see what a master of the genre could do when writing at the peak of his powers.

SUMMARY

This chapter has explored the paradoxical aspects of time travel to the past. The distinction between a time traveler *affecting* the past (OK) and *changing* the past (not OK) was emphasized. We dis-cussed the *grandfather paradox* in some detail, proving it to be a red herring. The *principle of self-consistency* is a crucial touchstone in any rational story, irrespective of genre, but it is particularly important in time travel tales. We also covered the mysterious causal loop paradoxes (particularly mysterious when just information circulates around a time loop), and one special category, the sexual paradoxes, was shown to be biologically impossible.

CHAPTER 9

Time Machines That Physicists Have Already 'Invented'

Within forty-eight hours we had invented, designed, and assembled a chronomobile. I won't weary you with the details, save to remark that it operated by transposing the seventh and eleventh dimensions in a hole in space, thus creating an inverse ether-vortex and standing the space-time continuum on its head.

from L. Sprague de Camp's "Some Curious Effects of Time Travel" (*Analog Readers' Choice* 1981); probably not the way to build a time machine.

No one yet, as far as I know, has built a time machine in real hardware. However, physicists have long known how to build such a gadget on paper. In fact, there are *several* different ways, but so far they all share one discouraging common feature—they require huge quantities of energy and/or similarly vast amounts of matter (perhaps even infinite amounts), under very strange conditions. These conditions are not necessarily impossible, but they are so unlike anything ever observed on Earth that they are lumped under the heading of "exotic" (which is, if anything, an understatement). In this chapter, I'll describe four such "paper" time machines.

First, let's take a look at black holes. General relativity predicts that a sufficiently massive star (greater than about four times the mass of the sun) will, when its fuel is nearly gone and its nuclear fires begin to fade, experience a truly spectacular death called gravitational collapse. When its fuel-exhausted, weakened radiation pressure is no longer able to keep an aged star inflated against the collapsing force of its own gravity, the star will literally implode and crush itself into what is called a *black hole* (a term coined in 1967 by the Princeton University physicist John Wheeler). This is an object with a gravitational field so enormous that even light cannot escape (hence the "black") and whose center is a singularity in space-time; this center would be a place where it seems space-time is either terribly weird or perhaps no longer exists. To quote Stephen Hawking, "A singularity is a place where the classical concepts of space and time break down, as do all the known laws of physics."

A singularity, according to general relativity, is infinitely dense and has a gravity field infinitely strong. The curvature of space-time at a singularity is infinite. The infinite "gravity graveyard" of a black hole is both exciting and suspicious. The infinity seems to be intertwined with time travel, but historically when such infinities have occurred in physical theories it has meant that the theories have been extended too far. The infinity may mean that once the collapsing star has fallen into a region incredibly smaller than even an electron, then Einstein's general relativity is no longer valid (just as Newton's theory fails at speeds comparable to that of light); if this is the case, under these conditions most if not all of its predictions are then wrong.

If, however, we stay away from the singularity, then general relativity is certainly correct. For example, around the singularity of a black hole, at a distance directly proportional to the mass of the collapsed object, the theory predicts the formation of a space-time *event horizon*, which is a surface in space-time through which anything can fall into the hole, but through which nothing, not even photons, can escape; the singularity at the center of a collapsed star, therefore, is not visible to the outside universe (i.e., it is not "naked"). For an observer beyond the event horizon of any black hole, the only observable properties are its mass (via its gravitational effects), angular momentum (its spin), and its electric charge.

There are, in fact, two fundamentally different kinds of black holes. If the collapsed star forms a nonrotating (i.e., zero angular momentum), spherically symmetric object, then it is called a *Schwarzschild* black hole, after the German astronomer Karl Schwarzschild (1873–1916), who found (before Einstein) the first exact solutions to Einstein's general relativity equations just months after Einstein published his theory. The radius of the space-time event horizon is called, in this case, the Schwarzschild radius. Curiously, Schwarzschild's result had been discovered earlier using Newton's theory of gravity, and the conclusion that there might be astronomical bodies from which not even light could escape was reported in a letter written in 1783 by the Reverend John Michell.

After Schwarzschild, the young Indian astrophysicist Subrahmanyan Chandrasekhar pioneered an analysis on the gravitational collapse of stars; in 1931, he combined special relativity and quantum mechanics to show that nonrotating stars above a certain mass (the *Chandrasekhar limit*) will experience a fate different from that of less massive stars. Beyond this limit of about 1.4 solar masses, a star cannot evolve into a white dwarf, something that before Chandrasekhar had been believed to be the ultimate fate of all stars. For this brilliant work, Chandrasekhar many years later shared the 1983 Nobel Prize in physics.

Interestingly, about the same time Chandrasekhar was reaching his results, Murray Leinster's classic science fiction tale "Sidewise in Time" expressed similar ideas (*Astounding Stories*, June 1934). This is primarily a parallel universe story (about which more is said in chapter eleven), but near its conclusion—in the obligatory "genius-explains-it-all" denouement (a weak writer's device that long ago fell out of favor)—we read:

We know that gravity warps space. . . . We can calculate the mass necessary to warp space so that it will close in completely, making a closed Universe . . . We know, for example, that if two gigantic star masses of certain mass were to combine . . . they would simply vanish. But they would not cease to exist. They would merely cease to exist in our space and time.

Another character in the story offers further explanation: It is "like crawling into a hole and pulling the hole in after you."

For our purposes, *rotating* black holes are much more interesting than Schwarzschild black holes. Rotating black holes are often called *Kerr holes*, after the New Zealand mathematician Roy Kerr who first solved the general relativity equations for the physics in the space-time region outside the event horizon of a spinning hole. A nonrotating black hole, which has a point singularity, cannot be used for time travel (but since angular momentum is always conserved, and since it is most unlikely that any pre-collapsed star would have exactly zero spin, it is very unlikely that a black hole would not be rotating).

A rotating Kerr hole, however, has a *ring* singularity through which a time traveler can theoretically pass (and thus avoid the deadly infinity of a point singularity) to enter other universes and/ or to time travel in this one. That is, there are other solutions to the gravitational field equations that imply that the interiors of such rotating holes are portals into space-time regions otherwise inaccessible from our universe, and that some of these regions are past (or future) versions of our universe. Such portals are the doors into time machines.

This is all very speculative, of course, and one objection to black-hole time travel is based on the *quantum field fluctuations* of gravity fields, which are related to the uncertainties inherent in our knowledge of the values of physical entities (this issue is raised again in chapter eleven in a discussion of quantum gravity). Such fluctuations, vanishingly small in systems of everyday size, increase dramatically at very tiny distances (such as twenty orders of magnitude smaller than the nucleus of an atom, where distance is measured in units of the Planck length, equal to 1.6×10^{-35} meters). These fluctuations might actually preclude the formation of the singularity. There does seem to be some astronomical evidence for black holes, but the question is not settled by any means and perhaps they don't actually exist. When the theory of quantum gravity is at last developed, we will learn if rotating black holes are really potential time machines.

The theoretical time travel property of rotating black holes once made them a favorite of science fiction writers, (e.g., Joe Haldeman's exciting 1984 novel *The Forever War*), but in my personal opinion they are no longer very credible candidates for time travel stories. Other time machines exist (on paper, remember) that are better candidates for your tales.

ROTATING CYLINDERS

In 1974, a young physics graduate student at the University of Maryland, Frank Tipler, caused a bit of a stir when he published what seemed to be the specific construction details for a time machine. Indeed, the final sentence of his paper (published in *Physical Review D*) reads, "In short, general relativity suggests that if we construct a sufficiently large rotating cylinder, we create a time machine." Nobody had ever made such a statement before in a respectable physics journal. Best of all, there were no apparent singularities as with black holes. However, a close look at Tipler's analysis does turn up a few difficulties.

Tipler actually had shown that if one had an *infinitely long, very dense* cylinder rotating with a surface speed of at least half the speed of light, then this would allow a closed timelike path to connect many otherwise unconnectable events in space-time. That means that by moving around the surface of such a fantastic cylinder, one could travel through time into the past—but not earlier than the creation date of the cylinder. Tipler's cylinder would also allow a time traveler to return to his original time, to go back to the future.

What happens with Tipler's cylinder is that its rapid rotation causes a distortion of space-time that "tips" light cones over; i.e., the *future* half of the light cone for an observer at one point in space-time can actually tip over enough to overlap the *past* half of the light cone for another point in space-time. You can visualize this by referring back to Figure 3.3 (on page 58) and imagining the light cones at two near-by points in space-time. Then, tipping (in your mind) each of the light cones over (say, 45° to the right), notice how the future half of one enters the past half of the other. It is difficult to say more about this without unleashing a lot of mathematics.

Light-cone "tipping" by a rotating mass is a theoretical result from general relativity that was discovered quite early (in 1918) by the Germans Josef Lense and Hans Thirring—it is often called, as you might expect, the Lense-Thirring effect. As the end result, the tipping creates paths in space-time that are always directed into the local future but which end up in the global past. At all times the world-line of a traveler along such a path is inside the future half of his present light cone (i.e., he never exceeds the speed of light, and his world-line is timelike). That is, the rotating cylinder has generated closed timelike curves in space-time. In other words, it has created a time machine. In fact, no one disputes this. It is true. On paper.

But Tipler did not prove that this time travel property holds for cylinders of long but finite length, which are the only kind we could actually build from a finite amount of matter: He merely *suggested* such might be the case. This suggestion seems reasonable, because if our time traveler orbits at the midpoint of the cylinder, near the surface, then the gravitational end-effects of the sufficiently remote ends of the cylinder could conceivably be negligible. Indeed, it has been estimated that a 10-to-1 ratio of cylinder length to radius may be enough for Tipler's cylinder to be "infinite." However, there is still a potential problem because there is a strong likelihood that a Tipler protocylinder would collapse under its own internal gravitational pressure before being made nearly long enough to be even approximately infinite. That is, such a finite-length cylinder might actually crush itself along its long axis into a pancake-shaped blob, something like what happens to a long cylinder of gelatin stood on end.

The required rotational speed causes a problem, too. We are, you see, not talking about cylinders the diameter of a pencil or even that of a large water pipe (the larger the diameter, the less the centrifugal acceleration at the cylinder's surface). It is easy to calculate that even a huge cylinder 10 kilometers in radius (and so at least 100 kilometers in length) would have, with a surface speed of half the speed of light, a centrifugal acceleration two hundred billion times the acceleration of Earth's surface gravity. No known form of ordinary matter could spin that fast and not explosively disintegrate.

But Tipler cylinders would not be ordinary in any sense of the word. Tipler has estimated that the required density for a time machine cylinder would be 40 to 80 orders of magnitude above that of nuclear matter. Made of such superdense stuff, a cylinder would typically be as massive as the sun but many trillion times smaller. Indeed, Tipler has written that whatever the constituents of these cylinders might be, it could only be called "unknown material." This requirement for supermatter seems to be a feature of time machines in general; black holes are obviously "weird," and as I'll discuss next, both the wormhole and cosmic-string time machines also require what are called "exotic conditions" for matter. Showing no lack of imagination, Tipler himself suggested the possibility of speeding up the rotation of an existing star as an alternative approach to actually trying to build a cylinder. This is, of course, a project for a far-future society with a very advanced technology.

So, while Tipler cylinders are out as practical time machines, at least for a while, Larry Niven liked the idea enough to lift the title of Tipler's original paper for his 1979 short time travel story "Rotating Cylinders and the Possibility of Causality Violation." Science fiction writer Poul Anderson had used Tipler cylinders even earlier (he called them "T-machines") in his 1978 novel *The Avatar*. He describes such cylinders as scattered about the universe by ancient, altruistic aliens called "The Others," to be used by anyone with the wits to understand their function. Anderson recognized the obvious problems with Tipler cylinders as he has one of his characters say, "I have no doubt whatsoever that here is the product of a technology further advanced from ours than ours is from the Stone Age."

WORMHOLES

The wormhole is the most likely to succeed of the paper designs that have been advanced for building a time machine, and it has already become quite popular among science fiction writers. It appears to be very exciting, too, for physicists. As one group of researchers wrote (in a 1990 issue of *Physical Review D*) after a mathematical demonstration that time travel by wormhole does not conflict with the conservation of energy, "This fact reinforces the authors' feeling that [closed time loops] are not so nasty as people generally have assumed."

Gödel rotated the entire universe in 1949 to achieve time travel, while Tipler reduced the problem in 1974 to merely spinning an infinite cylinder. In 1988, a group of CalTech physicists scaled things down even more, this time to the other extreme. Their idea calls for pulling a wormhole on the scale of the Planck length out of the quantum foam (see chapter eleven for more on this) that constitutes space-time, then somehow enlarging it to human scale, all the while stabilizing it against self-collapse, and finally using the time-dilation effect of special relativity to alter time at one mouth of the wormhole as compared to the other mouth. The rest of this chapter will explain what all this means.

Wormholes have actually been around in physics for decades, but had been thought to lack the stability to exist beyond paper, in the mathematics of general relativity. In one analysis published thirty-five years ago, for example, wormhole instability was shown to be so severe that not only would a human have no chance of getting through one, but not even a single speedy photon could do so. Even at the speed of light, the photon could not zip through a wormhole before being trapped inside ("pinched off") in a region of infinite space-time curvature. Wormholes would simply collapse too quickly after formation for even the so-called "ultimate speed" to save anything inside. Indeed, the presence of matter-energy inside a wormhole accelerates its collapse. The dynamics of wormholes, it had always seemed, made them simply untraversable.

Regardless, how would one get access to a wormhole in the first place? As suggested by the CalTech group, one might perhaps imagine someday finding a rotating (Kerr) black hole that mathematically possesses (in its interior solution) so-called hyperspace tunnels to other places—either in our universe or in other universes (see Figure 9.1). In the case of a wormhole connecting two places in the same universe, the external distance between the places may be very large (mega-light years) and the distance through the wormhole very small. The time required to traverse the wormhole, as measured by the traveler's watch, would be essentially zero. At the same time as they made this suggestion, the CalTech physicists also presented powerful arguments against the existence of Kerr wormholes and for why—if they do exist—they would be untraversable.

But all is not lost. These same scientists also showed that there are other exact solutions to the Einstein field equations that describe other kinds of hyperspace wormholes with none of the Kerr wormhole problems. Such problems include huge tidal forces that would tear would-be travelers to pieces, suggesting that the wormholes in such novels as Robert Wilson's *A Bridge of Years* (1991) and Murray Leinster's *Time Tunnel* (1964), through which people simply *walk*, are not what actual wormholes would be like. (See J.C. Wheeler's article referenced in the bibliography for a description of the details of how things would look *inside* a wormhole—in particular, you could not see through the tunnel-like wall because of the severe distortion effect on light by the extreme spacetime curvature of a wormhole.)

So, how do we get our hands on one of these traversable wormholes? The CalTech group is honest—they don't know. Their best suggestion is that "one can imagine an advanced civilization pulling [such] a wormhole out of the quantum foam and enlarging it to classical size." Then, once inflated, the wormhole could be stabilized

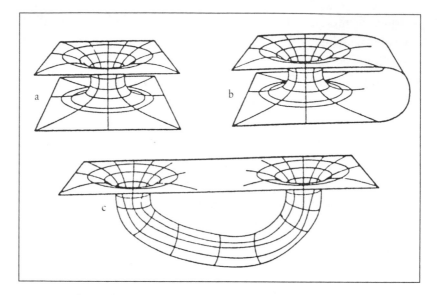

Fig. 9-1 These sketches are unavoidably misleading, being two-dimensional renditions of wormholes connecting two places in a three-dimensional space. Time machine wormholes, on the other hand, connect two places in four-dimensional space-time. In particular, the mouths of the wormholes will not appear to be depressions into which a time traveler's rocketship dives, but rather three-dimensional spheres. The wormhole in (a) connects two disjointed universes, while those in (b) and (c) are connections in the same universe. As shown in the last two cases, the wormhole "handle" can either be long or short compared to the distance in external or normal space between the wormhole mouths.

against collapse by threading it with either matter or fields of stupendous negative (outward) tension. And by stupendous, they mean *stupendous*. As the CalTech scientists showed, the tension (outward radial pressure) at the entry throat of a wormhole would be at least the same order of magnitude as the pressure at the center of the most massive neutron star. To stabilize a common sort of everyday "wormhole" like a subway tunnel, we can obtain the required tension/pressure by lining the tunnel with iron plates, but how do you line a hyperspace wormhole with iron plates that can achieve the required enormous pressure? Such superstuff could only be called "exotic."

EXOTIC MATTER, ENERGY CONDITIONS, AND GRAVITY TIME DILATION

As if all this isn't already complicated enough, another even more curious problem exists. The requirement that the wormhole interior smoothly connect to the external space-time demands that the wormhole throat flare outward, as shown in Figure 9.1. This condition is equivalent to requiring that the throat tension exceed the mass-energy density of the throat material. In turn, this requires that, for some observers, the throat mass-energy density must be negative. In other words, the material that makes up the throat has to be stronger than the material that makes up the rest of the wormhole. (The condition of the throat tension exceeding the mass-energy density of the wormhole throat material is, in fact, the technical definition of *exotic* material.) This can be interpreted as meaning that the exotic material keeps the wormhole mouth open by exerting a repulsive gravitational force.

Another interesting implication immediately follows. Just as Einstein's general relativity predicts that the sun's attractive gravitational field will bend starlight passing near the sun's edge *inward* (the *lensing effect*, verified in 1919), the repulsive field in the wormhole throat will cause any light rays traveling through the wormhole to bend *outward*. That is, a tight, narrow beam of radiation entering a wormhole will emerge defocused. This is crucial, in fact, as you'll soon see that otherwise the light from the dimmest candle could destroy a wormhole time machine.

At one time, it was almost a law of nature that no observer should ever be able to measure a negative mass-energy density (the *weak energy condition*), but that is now known to be false. The *strong energy condition* says gravity is always attractive, never repulsive; therefore both the weak and the strong energy conditions are violated by wormholes. But let's ignore all these problems and suppose instead that somehow we've managed to acquire a wormhole with both mouths in the same (our) universe. How can we imagine turn-ing it into a time machine?

Interestingly, while it is general relativity that gives us the wormhole, it is special relativity that adds the final touch of back-wards time travel. I'll begin by asking you to imagine that, somehow, one mouth of the wormhole can be moved with respect to the other mouth. For example, it has been suggested that if one mouth of the wormhole could be moved into the intense gravitational field of a nearby massive body (such as a neutron star), then *gravitational time dilation* would slow the rate of time at that mouth. This is an effect that has been observed on Earth (in extremely delicate experiments), and it is a direct consequence of relativity theory. This mechanism is the most likely to cause time dilation naturally in the universe. (Science fiction has not made much use of this effect, as far as I know, but one beautiful story that does is Poul Anderson's 1968 non-time-travel tale "Kyrie"; I found it in Volume 3 of the 1971 anthology *The Road to Science Fiction*.)

Alternatively, and most directly, one could use the gravitational interaction of a large asteroid to "drag" one end of the wormhole to create a motion-induced time dilation effect (recall, as discussed in chapter two, that a moving clock runs slow with respect to a station-ary clock). Now, suppose that we have two clocks A and B, one in each mouth of the wormhole. These two clocks, and other clocks in the space outside the mouths, are initially all running at the same rate and indicating the same time. Recalling the twin paradox (again, see chapter two), let each mouth-clock play the role of one of the twins. Imagine, that is, that clocks A and B are separated because mouth B (along with its clock) is placed on board a rocketship, which takes a long, high-speed trip out into space and then returns. We then unload mouth B from the rocketship and reposition it at its original location. What is the situation now?

We can summarize matters as follows:

(1) Clock A, in the nonmoving mouth, remains in step with the local clocks in the space outside the mouth.

(2) Clocks *A* and *B*, both inside the wormhole, have *not* moved with respect to each other because we are assuming a very short wormhole "handle" (as in part *a* of Figure 9.1). We can arrange for the motion of mouth *B* to be such that the handle is always short, and so the distance between clocks *A* and *B* changes by an arbitrarily small amount. Thus, clocks *A* and *B* remain "in step" with each other. Since the handle is always short, in wormhole space the clocks have not moved significantly and so cannot have experienced any time-dilation effects. For the clocks to have moved significantly, the handle would have to have grown in length. Therefore, if they were in step to start, they *remain* in step in their time-keeping.

(3) Clock *B*, because it has been moving with respect to the space outside of mouth *B*, arrives back at its starting point reading behind (i.e., earlier than) the clocks in the space outside of mouth *B*.

For the sake of being specific, suppose the journey of mouth *B* is such that there is a two-hour time-slip between clock *B* and the clocks outside of mouth *B* (remember, those outside clocks did *not* take the rocketship ride and so did not experience the time-slip). Thus, if clock *B* reads 9:00 A.M., the clocks outside of mouth *B* will read 11:00 A.M. But, since clocks *A* and *B* are in step, clock *A* also reads 9:00 A.M., as do the clocks outside of mouth *A*. That is, the wormhole connecting mouth *A* to mouth *B* is a connection between two parts of the same universe that are two hours apart in time.

Finally, suppose mouths *A* and *B* are positioned such that the journey from mouth *A* to mouth *B* can be made through *external space* in one hour. Then one could leave mouth *A* at 10:00 A.M., rocket to mouth *B* (or perhaps just walk, if both mouths are on Earth) by 11:00 A.M., enter mouth *B*, and travel back to mouth *A* via the wormhole to the starting point—where it is 9:00 A.M. (as established in the previous paragraph), one hour *before* the trip began. One can imagine repeating this entire process over and over, going backward in time one hour for each new loop through the wormhole. The wormhole works in the other direction, too. To see this, suppose the time traveler leaves mouth B at 8:00 A.M. and journeys to mouth A, arriving at 9:00 A.M. Entering mouth A, he exits from mouth B (where he started) at 11:00 A.M., two hours in the future.

CAUCHY AND CHRONOLOGY HORIZONS

Not everybody is convinced by these arguments, of course. They *are* pretty speculative. Physicists have long been bothered by the possible instability of what is called the *Cauchy horizon* (after a nineteenth-century French mathematician), the surface in space-time that separates the region where closed timelike curves can exist from the region where they cannot exist. (Recently, physicists have drawn a fine distinction between the Cauchy horizon, beyond which physics is unable to predict the future, and the *chronology* horizon, beyond which closed timelike curves exist. Often the two horizons are the same, but not always. For science fiction writing purposes, however, the distinction is not very important.) Radiation propagates in closed timelike loops that thread through the worm-hole on straight lines. The radiation can build to unbounded energy levels at the horizon, potentially destroying the horizon. This de-struction could occur if a single initial photon—what I earlier re-ferred to as the "dimmest candle"— were to "loop around time" endlessly until it multiplied itself to the energy level required to overwhelm the Cauchy horizon. Some disagree, however, arguing that the defocusing effect of a wormhole's exotic material could counter such an energy buildup.

Other speculations suggest that a wormhole transformed into a time machine by moving mouth B along a circular path (i.e., mouth B orbits mouth A to achieve time dilation) could avoid infinite en-ergy buildup at the Cauchy horizon. The idea is there would be no straight-line closed timelike loops threading such a wormhole from A to B because B would be a moving target, and there would not be a point of unbounded energy buildup on the horizon.

As mentioned earlier, wormholes have been around for a long time, both in physics and in science fiction. Recently, Gregory

Benford wrote a story about the discovery and capture of a worm-hole with one mouth in the sun ("A Worm in the Well," *Analog*, November 1995). Hollywood has also discovered wormholes, with films like the 1992 *Time Runner* and the 1994 *Stargate*.

COSMIC STRINGS

The last "paper" time machine I'll mention is the cosmic-string "machine," discovered in 1991 in the equations of general relativity by Princeton University physicist J. Richard Gott (see the article by Travis in the Bibliography). Cosmic strings are fantastically thin, threadlike structures of pure energy that are speculated to have been formed at the time of the Big Bang. According to present theory, they stretch the width of the universe, have a diameter mil lions of times smaller than that of the smallest atom, and have a linear mass-energy density on the order of several million billion tons per inch. Strings do not violate the weak energy condition, as wormholes do.

According to Einstein's general theory, pure energy has a gravitational field just as does mass; cosmic strings are so massive that their fields can warp (twist) space-time to an extreme degree. Gott showed that if two such very fast moving parallel strings (99.99999 percent of the speed of light) pass each other on a near collision course, their fields can warp space-time to the extent that closed timelike curves will encircle the strings.

Cosmic-string time machines have appeared in science fiction only once to my knowledge (Stephen Baxter's 1994 novel *Ring*), perhaps because they have some odd peculiarities that need to be addressed in a good hard science story. It has been shown, for example, that such a gadget cannot be built in an open (infinite) universe unless the total momentum of the universe is superluminal (or faster-than-light, a topic discussed at length in the next chapter). This is hard to imagine. Also, before the passing strings actually pass, the closed timelike curves they generate *start* at spatial infinity (so how can humans *control* them?) and collapse inward at the speed of light onto the interaction region of the strings (where they could be used by story characters—as in Baxter's novel—to travel through time). It is, admittedly, a bizarre concept; many physicists view cosmic-string time machines with suspicion, but it seems to me they are still great for science fiction. An author would have to explain how the approach of the two strings could be predicted to allow preparation for their use (in Baxter's novel *non*human, godlike beings create the string time machine). But that is quite restrictive—it represents a situation that has nothing to do with the creation of a time machine by human intelligence.

Of course, one can imagine ordinary human characters being accidently caught in a string near-miss or collapse (much like mountain climbers being swept away by an avalanche), so maybe there *is* a good time-travel story just waiting to be tied together with cosmic strings.

SUMMARY

This chapter described four theoretical mechanisms for achieving time travel (on paper), all of which have been used in science fiction: black holes; rotating cylinders; space-time wormholes; and cosmic strings. We discussed the pros and cons of all four time machines, with the emphasis on wormholes because they are the most likely of the four to someday actually work. The procedure for transforming a wormhole into a time machine uses time dilation induced by either motion (special relativity) or gravity (general relativity).

CHAPTER 10

Faster-Than-Light Into the Past

Velocities greater than that of light . . . have no possibility of existence.

Albert Einstein, 1905.

"We cannot fight the laws of nature."

"Nature be damned! Feed more fuel into the tubes. We must break through the speed of light . . . Give me a clear road and plenty of fuel and I'll build you up a speed of half a million miles a second. . . . What's there to stop it?"

words exchanged by the first officer and the captain of a starship on its way to Alpha Centauri in N. Schachner's "Reverse Universe." The captain, we are told, "had heard, of course, of the limiting velocity of light, but it meant nothing to him." (*Astounding Stories*, June 1936)

Some of the most intriguing paradoxes of time travel involve no traveler (at least no living one)—only information. Of course, any information flow at all involves the flow of energy and, as Einstein showed in his famous result in special relativity, energy and mass are different aspects of the same thing. Thus, information time travel involves the transfer of mass. So, a man in the twenty-fifth century sending a backward-in-time "temporal radio" message to a twentieth-century woman stating that he loves (will love?) her is sending much more than mere emotion (e.g., read Jack Finney's hard-to-find "The Love Letter" in *Tales Out of Time*—see the bibliography).

Two points should be clearly understood and kept in mind as you read this chapter. First, the Einstein quote that opens this chapter applies only to *local* regions of space-time, an area physicists would describe as a chunk of space-time sufficiently small that we can say it is *flat* and so the effects of space-time curvature (i.e., gravity) do not apply to it. A strong example would be a piece of land the size of a house lot which appears flat, even though the entire surface of the Earth is curved. In such a situation, special relativity (and the speed limitation) applies. On a global scale, however, where space-time curvature cannot be ignored, general relativity rules and faster-than-light speeds *are* possible, perhaps via wormholes.

Second, the paradoxes of information time travel arise only when backward time travel is involved. Writers do not always understand this fact, so let me say a little more on this point. Suppose a time traveler goes into the future and, before returning to his normal time, meets himself. Suppose further that the two quarrel and the time traveler kills his future-self. This is not paradoxical, but simply a delayed form of suicide. Now, suppose it is the time traveler that is killed. Then we have a variant of the grandfather paradox, and all the previous arguments against that red herring apply here, too. It is crucial to note that the very assumption that the time traveler finds an older self in the future implies that a backward journey will take place. This means that if a time traveler journeys forward and stays in the future, he simply will not find another, older version of himself there.

You have to keep all of the above ideas in mind when writing about information time travel, too. Now, all forms of present-day communication are transmissions only to the future. If you speak to someone or send a radio message, there are delays depending on the distance of separation and the speed of transmission of sound and of light, respectively. No new super-science technology is required to talk to the future. If you want a character in a story to send a message to the one-hundred-twenty-fifth century, you can very easily have him or her write a letter and seal it in a pressurized bottle of inert gas (e.g., helium). A version of this idea is in Murray Leinster's "Dear Charles" (in the 1960 collection *Time Twisters*), where a character in the twentieth century sends a message to the thirty-fourth century by simply printing it in a book that he knows will be preserved in a library. This is all quite ordinary, but certainly not in the reverse time direction.

What, for example, could be a more exciting message than the one received from the future by the young genius Cullen Foster, inventor of the first time machine in D. Stapleton's "How Much to Thursday?" (*Thrilling Wonder Stories*, December 1942)? After his initial experiment of sending the machine unmanned into the future, it returns with an envelope inside. Eagerly tearing it open, Foster finds a note from the National Academy of Sciences: "We know from old records and museum models that this is the Cullen Foster experimental machine. Fifty years looks down on you and says 'Good work'."

Heady stuff, but there are lots of other possible messages capable of competing with young Foster's in excitement. For example, suppose you had a gadget superficially similar to a telephone, but with the ability to call telephones in the distant future. You can hear the person (in the future) on the other end, but they can't hear you (in their past). That is, information can flow only from future to past. It is easy to create situations that at least seem paradoxical using this device. For example, suppose you call your own private number one month ahead. You hear your future self answer the phone and recite the winning lottery number for the "previous" day (but actually a month in your future). (Your future self recites the number because a month from now you will remember who is calling when your private phone rings.) So now the present you can make a fortune winning the lottery a month later. So far, of course, there is nothing paradoxical (or even illegal) in this—but what if, when the phone

rings in the future the day after you won the lottery, you then decide
not to read the winning number (this is called a *bilking paradox*)?

According to the block universe view of space-time, if the future
you spoke the lottery number, then the present you (a month later)
must inevitably read it. James Hogan's 1980 *Thrice Upon a Time* is
a novel-length discussion of a different view of the potential bilking
paradoxes produced by sending messages backward in time. The
puzzles presented are undeniably fascinating (and I highly recom-
mend the book), but Hogan's answer is to allow the changing of the
past. Indeed, the title comes from the plot device of twice changing
the past by sending messages backward in time to save the world
from terrible disasters (one of which is a swarm of micro black
holes in the Earth's interior.) One literally reads through entire time
periods three times before finishing the novel. As one character
declares, "We can monitor the actual consequences of our decisions
and actions, and change them until they produce the desired result!
My God . . . it's staggering!" Indeed, but there is nothing in today's
time machine research to support such a concept.

Back to my hypothetical gadget, let's suppose that instead of calling your future self you call the weather service and listen to the
recorded message telling you the weather thirty days hence. You
do this day after day, and after a while you get a reputation for being
able to predict, perfectly, the weather for every day to come up to
a month into the future. Your reputation spreads far and wide, and
after a while the weather service hears about you. They check and
find you're never wrong. Their computer models are only 80 percent
accurate out to three days, and for a week's prediction and beyond
the general public might as well flip a coin on whether or not it will
rain. But you are 100 percent correct out to ten times their maximum
range so they hire you—indeed, you also get the job of making
recordings for the daily weather. (The voice on the other end of the
gadget has sounded sort of familiar for the last month.) So here's
the puzzle, a nice little information causal loop—from *where* does
the information in the flawless weather prediction come? (This is
the same puzzle I hinted at in chapter eight, concerning the origin

of Dum's book on how to make a time machine.)

One easy answer to that last question is that it must be meaningless because such a future-to-the-past information flow would be impossible. At least it seems impossible for a writer to come up with an explanation for such a gadget. One solution is to simply avoid giving an explanation. Stan Schmidt elected to do so in his first-person, hard-boiled detective murder mystery "Worthsayer." The gadget in his tale is called a "time telephone," but he gives no theory for its operation. It is merely called a "straightforward application of an impressive, but limited, technology." (A grand, impressive understatement.) If Schmidt, who is presently editor of *Analog* and a Ph.D. physicist, had trouble explaining time telephones, maybe there really is a problem. Indeed, I must admit that one consistent, nonparadoxical answer is found in recognizing that I have assumed those thirty-day weather reports are correct, but maybe they are in fact no better than anybody else's predictions. So you don't become famous, and you don't get hired—and so there isn't any paradox. Is this the only answer to avoid paradoxes involving information flowing backward in time?

Perhaps not. As long ago as 1917, it was realized that special relativity does not preclude such an apparent backward flow. If information could be transmitted faster than light, then messages could travel backward in time. It was in that year that Richard Tolman, a professor of physical chemistry at the University of Illinois and later CalTech, wrote (in his book *The Theory of the Relativity of Motion*): "The question naturally arises whether velocities which are greater than that of light could ever possibly be obtained." He then answered this question, with his general conclusion being that if such velocities are possible, then an observer moving faster than light (FTL) could see the time order of two causally connected events reverse. That is, the observer would see the result occur before the cause. This has come to be called *Tolman's paradox*, although Professor Tolman himself was careful with his words: "Such a condition of affairs might not be a logical impossibility; nevertheless, its extraordinary nature might incline us to believe that no causal impulse can travel with a velocity greater than that of light."

(An aside: Even though "faster than light" means "backward in time," which means "causality failure," as I'll soon show you, special relativity still holds true and nothing awful happens to physics [only to our everyday intuitions, which means our intuitions are wrong, not the physics]. The reason being that causality, contrary to common belief even among some physicists who should know better, is not a premise or starting point of special relativity.)

Tolman's paradox is an extraordinary result, but it has in fact been extended to state that the time order of two noncausal events can appear reversed not only for a subluminal observer, but also to a reversal of causally related events for a superluminal observer. That is, faster-than-light (FTL) motion and time travel to the past go hand-in-hand. Even today, this conclusion is not always appreciated by writers. For example, consider the otherwise elegant horror story by Randall Garrett, "Time Fuze," which plays with one of the implications of being able to outrun light. It unfortunately overlooks the time travel issue. In this tale, FTL spaceships have a fatal flaw— their use induces nearby stars (including the sun) to go nova. Because the first such ship outpaced the light of the sun's explosion on the departure of its maiden flight, the crew doesn't see the resulting destruction of the entire solar system until their return.

One can reverse (at least conceptually) the sequence and achieve FTL speed via time travel. To go from A to B at FTL speed, just follow this procedure: Put yourself in hibernation at A; cruise as slowly as you'd like in a spaceship to B; wake up, get into your time machine and travel backward in time as far as the temporal duration of your cruise (as measured by your wristwatch). This actually lets you achieve infinite speed. Going back in time a little bit more means, of course, that you arrive at B before you leave A. This idea has been used in science fiction; e.g., see Theodore R. Cogswell's "Minimum Sentence."

The obvious question at this point, of course, is to ask if it is even conceptually possible to build a gadget to send FTL signals backward in time? Well, back in the early 1940s Richard Feynman (a 1965 co-winner of the Nobel Prize in physics, but then still a graduate student at Princeton) and his advisor John Wheeler devised a theory for radio waves that travel backward in time. This is technically called the *advanced solution* to Maxwell's equations for the electromagnetic field, but it hasn't found much use in science fiction.

The only story I know that has specifically used Feynman and Wheeler's idea is John Robinson Pierce's "Pre-Vision" (*Astounding Stories*, March 1936), in which a gadget (using what Pierce called the "anticipated potentials") can display the future on a TV-like screen. The author's byline on this tale proudly gives his academic credentials as the holder of a master's degree, and John Robinson Pierce was a graduate student in electrical engineering at CalTech. As an electrical engineering student, Pierce knew all about Maxwell's equations, and indeed his story actually opens with a quote from a 1924 article in the technical journal *The Physical Review* on the advanced solution. This is a great example of how being familiar with technical literature can be of help to the science fiction writer looking for new ideas. (See chapter twelve for more on this point.)

Perhaps the most interesting science fiction use of backward-in-time signaling is James Blish's classic, "Beep." Blish describes the "Dirac radio" for instantaneous transmissions (after the real-life English mathematical physicist Paul Dirac, who shared the 1933 Nobel Prize in physics for his brilliant work in quantum mechanics), and we learn that at the beginning of each received message there is always an irritating audio beep (hence the title) that is a seemingly useless artifact of the mysterious workings of the Dirac radio.

Blish's beep has a continuous frequency spectrum from 30 hertz to well above 18,000 hertz (your telephone, as an example, reproduces sound from about 300 to 3,000 hertz), but it is only at the end of the tale that the central character in the story learns that this spectrum is the "simultaneous reception of every one of the Dirac messages that have ever been sent, or will be sent." (I should tell you that electrical engineers will immediately nod their heads in agreement with this nice little technical touch by Blish, as the jumbled overlap of countless unrelated signals would indeed result in the continuous spectrum of the "beep.") There is no mention of Wheeler and Feynman's advanced waves, but clearly Blish knew that instantaneous (i.e., infinite velocity) signals would travel into the past (as you'll soon see). The story does a masterful job of presenting the mystery of listening to the far future. At one point, for example, characters in the twenty-first century hear the commander of a time-traveling "world-line cruiser" transmit a poignant call for help from 11,000,000 light-years away, and from sixty-five centuries in the future.

TACHYONS AND SPECIAL RELATIVITY

Science fiction writers have often used FTL motion to reverse time. For example, in Stanley Weinbaum's "The Worlds of If" there is this throwaway line in a lecture on time travel from a curmudgeonly (but lovable) old physics professor, Haskel van Manderpootz: "And as for the past—in the first place, you'd have to exceed light-speed, which immediately entails the use of more than an infinite number of horsepowers." Take another look at chapter two, on how mass increases to infinity as speed approaches that of light, to see what Manderpootz means. This is the second reason beyond the reversal of cause and effect, for many physicists' rejection of backward time travel, irrespective of the paradox issues. FTL motion implies travel to the past, but such FTL motion is impossible precisely because of the infinite energy required by special relativity to penetrate the light barrier so time travel to the past must be impossible, too.

Professor Manderpootz's point is a good one. (It comes straight from Einstein, as seen in the opening quote of this chapter.) Nevertheless, there may be a way around his argument. The key to a possible rebuttal depends on the existence of particles that do not need to be accelerated up to and through the light barrier because they are, at the instant of creation, already FTL. Such particles are the now well-known *tachyons*, whose name was coined by the late American physicist Gerald Feinberg in 1967 from the Greek word *tachys* for "swift." (Feinberg once admitted his interest in FTL particles and backward-in-time messages was originally sparked by reading Blish's "Beep.")

Relativity theory precludes the acceleration of a massive particle to the speed of light, but does allow a massless particle (the photon) to exist just at the speed of light. Photons are emitted during various physical processes, and they move at the speed of light from the instant of their creation; the only way to slow a photon down is to destroy it by absorbing it. Advocates of the possible existence of tachyons make a similar argument by suggesting that there might be particles emitted during various physical processes (yet unknown) that move from the instant of their creation at speeds greater than that of light. Such an argument neatly avoids the "acceleration through the light-barrier" problem mentioned by Manderpootz. But even with that problem out of the way, other concerns must be considered.

For example, tachyons would have to have *imaginary rest mass*. (Look back, again, at the mass equation in chapter two and you'll see that if the particle speed, v, exceeds the speed of light, c, we get the square root of a negative number—and what in the world could that possibly mean? This issue is related to the reason why such things as the intersection point of two very long, closing scissor blades can easily exceed the speed of light—such a point, which exists only in our minds, is massless and, even more importantly, transports no energy.) One possible answer is that the rest mass of a superluminal particle is actually unobservable because there is no subluminal reference frame in which such a speedy particle could be at rest. That is, there is no frame of reference in which the mysterious imaginary mass could actually be measured (i.e., be seen), and it is only observable effects that are of interest in physics.

THE REINTERPRETATION PRINCIPLE AND ANTITELEPHONES

A more serious problem for tachyons, according to those physicists who dislike the idea of sending messages backward in time, is that in some frames of reference an FTL particle would appear to have

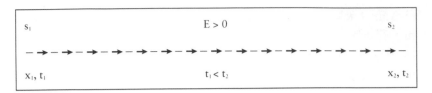

Fig. 10-1 Emission of a positive energy particle, followed by absorption.

negative energy. The reason why this is a problem comes from relativity itself, which says that any state that is possible for one observer must be possible for all observers ("there are no privileged observers"), and hence FTL particles could exist in negative-energy states for all observers. And the occurrence of negative-energy states for particles has traditionally been objected to on the grounds that it would lead to unstable, unphysical behavior in any nearby system that absorbed tachyons. This objection to FTL particles was raised early in the history of tachyon discussions, and it was answered by the so-called *reinterpretation principle.*

To see how the reinterpretation principle (which I'll now call simply the RP) works, consider Figure 10.1, which shows a tachyonic source S_1 located at x_1 emitting a tachyon particle at time t_1. This particle then travels to an absorber S_2 located at x_2, arriving there at the later time t_2. S_1 and S_2 are in the same reference frame, and for an observer in that frame the particle energy E is positive. So far, so good. However, it is always possible to find another observer in a relatively moving frame for whom this emission/absorption process would look as if t_2 were less than (i.e., before) t_1, with E negative. In other words, the moving observer would see the tachyon traveling backward in time with negative energy. But, while this admittedly sounds bizarre, the RP says it all makes sense.

Note that for the moving observer, the emission by S_1 of negative energy increases the energy of S_1, and the absorption of negative energy by S_2 decreases the energy of S_2. The decrease of S_2's energy occurs (for the moving observer) before the increase in energy by S_1 because (as above) t_2 is less than (before) t_1. The moving observer naturally interprets this process as the emission of positive energy by S_2, followed by absorption of the energy (the tachyon) by S_1. This reinterpretation of what has happened preserves, so it would seem, the commonsense idea of causality and avoids any mention of backward time travel. The RP appears to have slipped around these concerns by merely redefining which S is transmitting, and which is receiving, the tachyon.

The RP quickly appeared, in a garbled way, in science fiction. In Glen Cook's 1985 novel *A Matter of Time*, a physicist at one point says, "A few years ago there was a flap over a hypothetical particle called a tachyon. At first it was supposed to move faster than light and have negative mass. Then it was supposed to have positive mass and a velocity below that of light, but was supposed to moving backward in time." If Cook really meant to write that, then he simply failed to understand the distinction between negative and imaginary mass, as well as the RP itself.

THE FTL SIGNED MESSAGE PUZZLE

The RP's effect of flipping the roles of transmitter and receiver does have problems, however. Some physicists have pointed out that if one can modulate (i.e., impose information onto) a superluminal signal to send a message into the past, then certainly one could sign the message. Since the RP cannot alter a signature, then the origin of the message is always completely unambiguous. To quote a delightful example from a famous technical analysis of this very point ("The Tachyonic Antitelephone," *Physical Review D*, July 15, 1970, pp. 263–265), "If Shakespeare types out *Hamlet* on his tachyon transmitter, Bacon receives the transmission at some earlier time. But no amount of reinterpretation will make Bacon the author of *Hamlet*. It is Shakespeare, not Bacon, who exercises control over the content of the message." This last line is of central importance. The authors (one of whom is Greg Benford, a science fiction writer and physics professor) emphasize its point by immediately observing that a signature is a relativistic invariant, and that, indeed, it establishes a causal ordering quite independent of any apparent temporal ordering.

THE SPACE-TIME GEOMETRY OF FTL

Finally, let me show you how all the space-time ideas developed in earlier chapters quickly and easily establish the intimate link between FTL motion and backward time travel. To do this, it will be useful to establish a geometrical interpretation of the Lorentz transformation. As discussed back in chapter two, if x', t' system is moving with speed v in the x (also the x') direction relative to the x, t system, then the Lorentz transformation equations are:

$$x' = [x - vt]/LF$$
$$\text{and}$$
$$t' = [t - vx/c^2]/LF$$

where LF denotes the "Lorentz factor," i.e.,

$$LF = \sqrt{1 - (v/c)^2}.$$

These equations make sense for $v < c$, and I will retain this condition for the two relatively moving reference frames in all that follows. That is, our human observers will always be subluminal. I'll use the new symbol w to denote the speed of an FTL particle.

With reference to Figure 10.2, recall what we mean by saying a line is parallel to the x axis: It is a line with a fixed time coordinate. Such a line is a cosmic moment line, with the equation $t = $ constant. Similarly, for the moving system we would write the equation of a cosmic moment line as $t' = $ constant which, after using the Lorentz transformation, you can see is equivalent to:

$$t - (vx/c^2) = \text{constant}.$$

In particular, the x' axis (the $t' = 0$ cosmic moment line), which passes through the point $x = 0$, $t = 0$, has the equation:

$$t = (vx)/c^2 = vx.$$

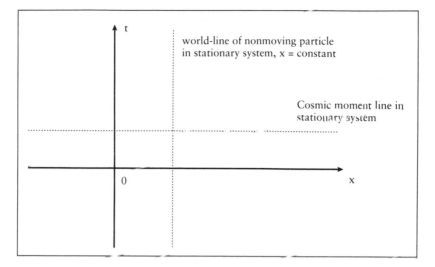

Fig. 10-2 Lines parallel to the time and space axes in a stationary system.

This follows if we use the usual convention of taking $c = 1$, i.e., all subluminal speeds are normalized with respect to the speed of light and so have values between 0 and 1.

In the same way, recall what we mean by saying a line is parallel to the t axis: It is a line with a fixed space coordinate. Such a line is the world-line of a stationary particle in the x, t frame, with the equation $x =$ constant. Similarly, for the moving system we would write $x' =$ constant as the equation of a stationary particle's world-line. From the Lorentz transformation, you can see this is equivalent to:

$$x - vt = \text{constant.}$$

In particular, the t' axis (which is the $x' = 0$ world-line of a particle stationary at the origin of the moving system) passes through the $x = 0$, $t = 0$ point, and it has the equation:

$$x = vt.$$

Thus, superimposed space-time coordinate axes for the two frames look like Figure 10.3. The relative motion of the two frames

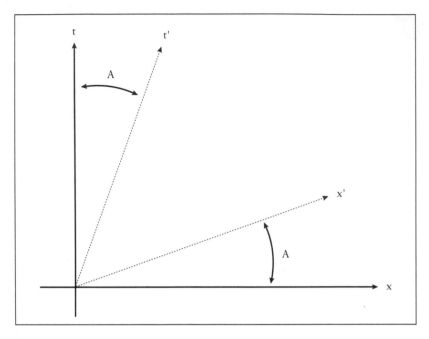

Fig. 10-3 Space-time coordinate rotation by relative motion.

results in a rotation of the space-time axes; but it is a strange sort of rotation, with opposite rotation directions for the space and the time axes. The x' and the t' axes make equal angles A with the x and t axes, respectively, and if we limit the moving frame to subluminal speeds (i.e., $0 < v < 1$), then $0 < A < 45°$. At the speed of light ($v = 1$) we have $A = 45°$, and the x' and t' axes coincide—time and space have become indistinguishable.

It is important to realize that observers in either system would measure the same speed for a photon; each would see the world-line of a photon as a line with slope 1. This result is, in fact, literally built into the Lorentz transformation because one of Einstein's fundamental postulates for special relativity is the invariance of the speed of light. The truth of this assertion for the x, t system is obvious using the space-time diagram. It is, perhaps, not so obvious with the x', t' system because of the nontraditional, nonperpendicular axes (as drawn on paper) in that system. In Figure 10.4, the world-line of a photon is shown in both systems. In the figure, imagine that

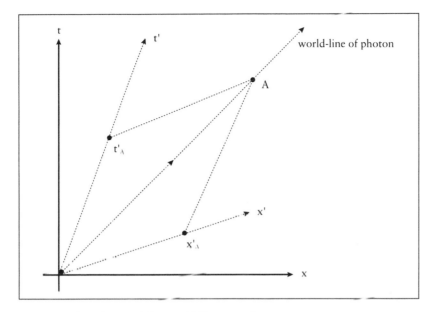

Fig. 10-4 Invariance of the world-line of a photon.

we emit a photon at $x' = 0$, $t' = 0$ and later measure its coordinates at point A to be $x' \neq x'_A$ at time $t' = t'_A$. Notice carefully how this is done. I've drawn lines from point A parallel to the x' and t' axes until they intersect the t' and x' axes, respectively. This is similar to finding the space-time coordinates of A in the more familiar x, t system, where you would draw lines parallel to the x, t axes.

It should now be obvious that x'_A and t'_A have the same extension, just as in the unprimed system, and so:

$$x'_A / t'_A = 1, \text{ the speed of light.}$$

The speed of light is the only invariant speed under Lorentz transformation. Indeed, the modern approach to special relativity emphasizes this invariance, rather than the idea of the speed of light as a limiting speed, as the central property of the speed of light.

This geometrical interpretation of the Lorentz transformation lets us quickly make another interesting (and, I think, not very obvious) observation: If a particle is faster than light in the x, t system, then

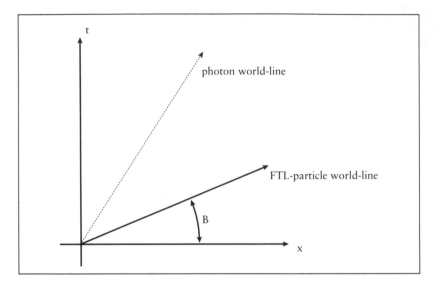

Fig. 10-5 World-line of a faster-than-light particle.

there exists a subluminal x', t' system for which the particle is infinitely fast. Figure 10.5 shows the world-line of an FTL particle in
the x, t system. (It is, of course, drawn below the world-line of a
photon.) Suppose the FTL particle has speed $w > c$, and that its
world-line makes angle B with the x-axis. If you now pick v, the
speed of the moving x', t' system, to be such that $A = B$, then the
x' axis will coincide with the world-line of the particle and the particle
will appear to an observer in the x', t' system to be "everywhere at
once," i.e., to be infinitely fast. You can show with just a little more
math (which is not necessary here), and unnormalizing v with respect to c (that is, putting c back in the expression for v, and not
assuming $c = 1$), that this happens at the critical speed:

$$v = c^2/w.$$

You can, of course, turn this result around. If an FTL particle
moves with speed w in the x, t system, then to an observer in the
x', t' system moving with subluminal speed v, the particle will appear
to be infinitely fast if $w = c^2/v$. A particle with $w > c^2/v$ is said to be
not just superluminal (FTL) but *ultraluminal*.

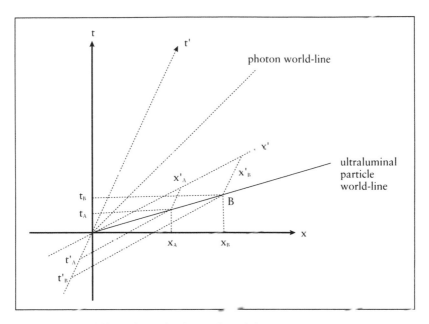

Fig. 10-6 World line of an ultraluminal particle.

Now for the obvious question. If a particle has infinite velocity with $w = c^2/v$, what happens if w is even larger? The answer is easy to see in a space-time diagram, as in Figure 10.6 where the x' and t' axes have been extended backward to negative values. In that figure, I have labeled two arbitrary events A and B on the worldline of an ultraluminal particle (which thus lies below the x' axis) and have plotted their space-time coordinates in both the x, t and x', t' systems. For the x, t system you can see that A is related to B by the relations $x_A < x_B$ and $t_A < t_B$; i.e, the particle is moving forward in time from A to B and is moving in space along the increasing x axis. However, in the x', t' system, A is related to B by the relations, $x'_A < x'_B$ and $t'_B < t'_A$, i.e., the time order of A and B is reversed for an observer in the x', t' system. To this observer, the particle appears to be traveling backward in time.

Consider the following situation, which uses the RP to create a causal information paradox. As shown in Figure 10.7, this example has an ultraluminal particle emitted by observer P at A at time $t = 0$ in the stationary frame of reference. For P, this particle is moving

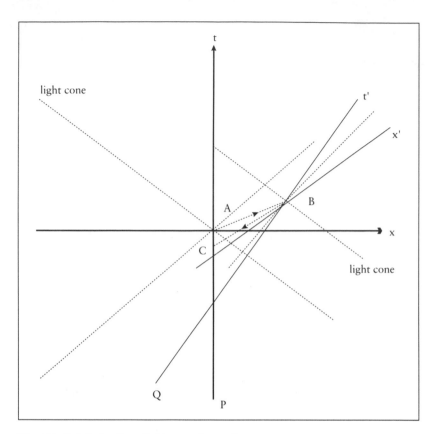

Fig. 10-7 A faster-than-light causal paradox.

forward in time and along the *x* axis in the positive direction. A relatively moving observer (call her Q) receives this particle at *B*. As mentioned earlier, what Q actually sees is a negative energy particle absorbed at *B*, but because of the RP she interprets it as if it were a positive energy particle emitted at *B* and traveling back down the *x'* axis in the negative direction.

Suppose at the instant Q observes the emission, she emits a second tachyon that goes even faster down the negative *x'* axis (this tachyon is more ultraluminal than the one originally emitted at *A*). This tachyon is then absorbed at *C*, an event observed by a past version of P, since *C* occurs earlier on the *t* axis than does *A*. P sees the second tachyon as a negative energy particle, of course, and (again because of the RP) he interprets it as the emission of a positive energy particle. The emission of this tachyon at $t < 0$ has been caused by the emission of the original tachyon at $t = 0$. Thus, we have backward causation because of the RP, with P seeing something happen at $t < 0$ because of something he will do at $t = 0$.

Of course, the problem now is the threat of a bilking paradox. After P sees the $t < 0$ event, suppose that he then does not emit the original tachyon? In fact, the authors of the 1970 "tachyonic antitelephone" paper I mentioned earlier use this very puzzle to conclude their presentation. They assume that there are two people, A and B, who each possess a tachyonic transmitter that can send messages backward in time by one hour: "Suppose A and B enter into the following agreement: A will send a message at three o'clock if and only if he does not receive one at one o'clock. B sends a message to reach A at one o'clock immediately on receiving one from A at two o'clock. Then the exchange of messages will take place if and only if it does not take place."

For a masterful treatment in the fictional use of tachyons to send messages backward in time, you should read Gregory Benford's 1980 *Timescape*, a novel in which the future tries to warn the past of impending disaster. Benford is highly effective in handling the issue of changing the past. Because he is a physicist by day, Benford knew he would have to address that point. He did so with quantum mechanics and splitting universes (a radical idea in 1980); these are topics that we will cover in the next chapter.

SUMMARY

At the beginning of this chapter, we discussed the issues concerning sending information through time, both to the future (as easy as writing a letter) and to the past (requires a time machine). Our next topic was the possibility of faster-than-light (FTL) speeds, a condition that is *not* forbidden by any of the postulates of special relativity. We studied the direct connection between time travel to the past and FTL motion, with each implying the other. An alternative theory for sending signals into the past, the so-called *advanced solution* to Maxwell's electromagnetic field equations, was presented; it was used in a science fiction story as early as 1936. Faster-than-light tachyons and the reinterpretation principle were our next topic, along with their uses in science fiction. The chapter concluded with a discussion of the paradoxes of sending signals into the past with tachyons.

CHAPTER 11

Quantum Gravity, Splitting Universes, and Time Machines

Space-time is friable. Wormholes riddle the fabric of space-time on all scales. At the Planck length and below, wormholes arising from quantum uncertainty effects blur the clean Einsteinian lines of space-time. And some of the wormholes expand to the human scale and beyond—sometimes spontaneously, and sometimes at the instigation of intelligence.

from Stephen Baxter's imaginative *Timelike Infinity*, his 1993 novel of a far-future alien civilization able to control the energies of *constellations* of galaxies.

A fundamental objection to time travel, based ironically on general relativity itself (which is our theoretical basis for time travel), is that, in a very deep sense, general relativity is known to be an incomplete theory. That is, it is incompatible with quantum mechanics. Quantum mechanics is the physics of very, very small structures, smaller even than a single molecule. On the other hand, classical physics, which works pretty well in the everyday macroscopic world, doesn't do anything right in the micromicroscopic world. In quantum mechanics, however, we find the explanation for why the discrete world of atomic phenomena is as it is: For example, the photoelectric effect (for which Einstein received the 1921 Nobel Prize in physics) where light is understood in terms of individual particles (photons) and not as the continuous waves of Maxwell's electromagnetic theory.

General relativity works beautifully on a cosmological scale but, like Maxwell's theory of electromagnetism and Newton's laws of mechanics, it fails utterly when applied to atoms. Quantum theory, on the other hand, seems to work everywhere. As physicist Nick Herbert writes in his excellent 1987 book *Faster Than Light*, "As far as we can tell, there is no experiment that quantum theory does not explain, at least in principle. . . . Though physicists have steered quantum theory into regions far distant from the atomic realm where it was born, there is no sign on the horizon that it is ever going to break down . . ."

THE UNCERTAINTY PRINCIPLE

As I introduced early in this book, one of the central concepts in relativity is the *world-line*, which is the complete story of a particle in space-time. A world-line assigns a definite position to the particle at each instant of time. This is a classical, prequantum image, however, and today physicists use the probabilistic ideas of quantum mechanics to describe the position and momentum (essentially the direction and speed) of a particle when they get down to the atomic level. As mentioned briefly back in chapter nine, the famous *uncertainty principle* of Heisenberg says that there are definite limitations on how precisely we can know both the position and momentum of a particle.

Quantum theory is a discrete theory, in which the values of physical entities vary discontinuously (in "quantum jumps"), while in classical (i.e., pre-twentieth-century) theories, the values of physical entities are smoothly continuous (think of the difference between sand and water). Indeed, these two images of reality are so much at odds with each other that physicists who have tried to mix the two theories, general relativity and quantum mechanics, joke that all they end up with is suffocating quicksand.

In certain special cases, the joining of general relativity and quantum mechanics has already been accomplished. In 1974, Stephen Hawking announced an astonishing partial connection of quantum mechanics with general relativity's black holes. Hawking showed that black holes actually must radiate energy, contrary to the usual image of black holes as being one-way trap doors to . . . (who knows?). His analysis, which stunned physicists by its beautifully simple arguments, invokes Werner Heisenberg's uncertainty principle, one of the cornerstones of quantum physics (for which Heisenberg won the 1932 Nobel Prize). Hawking himself wrote that he found this result "greatly surprising."

The uncertainty principle states that there are certain pairs of variables associated with particles that cannot simultaneously be measured exactly. Time and energy are such a pair; i.e., a nonzero time interval is required to measure a particle's energy, and the product of the uncertainty in both the interval and the energy must be equal to or greater than a certain nonzero constant (Planck's constant, about 6.6×10^{-34} joule-second; the *joule* is a unit of energy, and a joule per second is one watt). This allows the process of *virtual particle creation*, the appearance of particle/antiparticle pairs just outside the surface of a black hole. The uncertainty in energy that is available to give the combined mass of the particles (remember, $E = mc^2$) is the so-called *quantum fluctuation energy* of the intense gravity field around the hole. The only constraint is that the energy be returned to the field (via mutual annihilation of the matter/anti-matter pair) within the time uncertainty dictated by Heisenberg.

As Hawking showed, that time interval, although incredibly short, is still long enough for the two virtual particles to separate

before annihilation, with one falling into the hole and the other es-
caping into space. By this incredible quantum process, then, the
black holes of general relativity slowly evaporate as they glow with
what is now called *Hawking radiation.* That is, quantum mechanics
says black holes should actually appear to be hot, emitting bodies.
But hot is relative; as Hawking also showed, a black hole with the
mass of the sun would appear to be a body with a temperature just
one microdegree Kelvin above absolute zero. That's pretty damn
cold, but it isn't *zero*, which is what everybody before Hawking had
thought.

The uncertainty principle has long been used in time travel science fiction. In W. Bade's 1951 story "Ambition," for example, a
character is transported from 1950 to 2634 by a scientist of the future. Once there, this character decides he'd like to remain perma-
nently in the twenty-seventh century. He is told he can't, because
he is like an atom excited into an elevated energy state. And just as
quantum mechanics predicts that eventually an electron in such an
atom will "drop back down" into a lower energy state (giving up its
excess energy as an emitted photon), so do the "laws of time travel"
require that he "drop back" to his normal time. How long can he
remain in the future, he is told, "depends on the mass [energy] of
his body and the number of years the mass [energy] is displaced."
This is simply another way of stating the uncertainty principle.

More sophisticated is the Nebula-winning story "Ripples in the
Dirac Sea" by physicist Geoffrey Landis, which uses Dirac's theory
of negative energy particles to explain the story's time machine.
The problem of the conservation of mass/energy in time travel (discussed in chapter six) is partially avoided in this tale by Landis's
"rule of time travel" that requires each visitor to the past to return
to the exact moment of departure (and this, in turn, is the basis for
the development of a highly original "trapped in time" idea, one
with enormous emotional tension that unfortunately is not relevant
here). Landis's rule means, of course, that in a certain sense the
mass/energy of the time traveler never left the present. And as
for the arrival of the mass/energy in the past, Landis explains that

problem with reference to the temporary borrowing of energy from the infinite Dirac sea of negative energy particles via the Heisenberg uncertainty principle, in a way similar to what Hawking did for virtual particle creation at the space-time horizon of a black hole.

The generalized unification of general relativity with quantum mechanics (to give what is called *quantum gravity*) has what could be very big implications for time travel. Consider these words by Martin Gardner, from *Scientific American*, March 1979 (in Gardner's "Mathematical Games" essay on time travel): "In all time-travel stories where someone enters the past, the past is necessarily altered. The only way the logical contradictions created by such a premise can be resolved is by positing a Universe that splits into separate branches the instant the past is entered." I think Gardner is mistaken when he says this because he has failed to properly distinguish between changing and affecting the past. But, no matter, his last line *is* intriguing—but what does he mean by it?

SPLITTING REALITIES

In fact, science fiction had, long before 1979, used this imagery of splitting universes to allow backward time travel and a changeable past while still avoiding paradoxes. The idea is that if a time traveler journeys into the past and introduces a change (indeed, his very journey alone may be the change) then, as Gardner stated, reality splits into two versions. One fork represents the result of the change, and the other fork the original reality before the change. (To a fifth-dimensional observer, of course, all possible forks, all possible four-dimensional space-times, have always existed). With this view the entire universe is splitting, every microinstant, along every alternative decision path for every particle. This is often called the *theory of alternate realities with parallel time tracks* in science fiction.

This fantastic view seems to actually have some scientific plausibility to it, too, because of the so-called *many-worlds interpretation of quantum mechanics*, pioneered by Hugh Everett III in his 1957 Princeton University doctoral dissertation (his advisor was the ubiquitous John Wheeler of black hole fame, who was also Richard Feynman's advisor in the early 1940s when antimatter as time-traveling ordinary matter was devised). Most physicists and philosophers don't like the idea of splitting universes, and to read their analyses of it is to read, over and over, such phrases as "highly controversial," "outlandish," "a bizarre notion," "ontologically bloated," and "the idea of 100^{100} slightly imperfect copies of the Universe all constantly splitting into further copies is not easy to reconcile with common sense. Here is schizophrenia with a vengeance." Even Everett's own advisor has backed away from the idea—in 1979 Wheeler wrote, "I once subscribed to it. In retrospect, however, it looks like the wrong track . . . its infinitely many unobservable worlds makes a heavy load of metaphysical baggage."

At least one science fiction writer had said the same thing, years before Wheeler's comment. In Bob Shaw's "What Time Do You Call This?," the inventor of the "chronomotive impulse belt" (which allows its wearer to move between the two parallel worlds that are all that exist) calls the many-worlds idea the "Doctrine of Infinite Redundancy—which is, of course, utter nonsense." This story mixes parallel worlds with splitting worlds, unfortunately, and the two are actually very different concepts. The idea of parallel worlds is that all possibilities have always existed, independent and parallel in time. From world to world there are copies of the same individuals, just like in splitting universes, but these copies have *not* split off from earlier versions in some other time line.

Everett's theory is the antithesis of what is commonly called the "collapse of the wave function," the idea that all potential possibilities have a nonzero probability until a consciousness actually decides or observes which one will be. This quantum-mechanical concept gets its name from the probability wave equation due to the physicist Irwin Schrödinger (who received the 1933 Nobel Prize in physics for this work). Before the observation, all possible futures have various values of probability; after the observation (which collapses the wave function described in Schrödinger's wave equation), one of the futures (the future) has probability one and all the others have probability zero. Science fiction quickly incorporated this dramatic imagery in such now-classic tales as Jack Williamson's 1939 novel *The Legion of Time* and C.L. Moore's 1939 short story "Tryst in Time."

L. Sprague de Camp was an early experimenter with a different idea in time-travel science fiction; e.g., in his classic 1941 novel *Lest Darkness Fall* he uses the analogy of a tree (the "main time line") that is always sprouting new branches (of time lines along new realities). That is, as in Everett's many-worlds interpretation, the wave function of the Universe does not collapse. Indeed, it couldn't, as there is no observer external to the entire Universe to observe the Universe. Instead, the wave function splits at every decision point in space-time. Although this leads to a multitude of realities beyond comprehension, cosmologists like it because it avoids the puzzle of an observer outside the Universe (God?).

But the cosmologists are in the minority among physicists on this point. For most, the underlying scientific theory of time travel is classical (i.e., nonquantum) general relativity, and that theory has nothing to say about alternate time tracks and parallel, splitting worlds. The late, great quantum physicist John S. Bell (in a famous essay called "Quantum Mechanics for Cosmologists") wrote this of the Everett theory: "If such a theory were taken seriously, it would hardly be possible to take anything else seriously." Bell points out in his essay that another implication of the many-worlds interpretation is that "there is no association of the particular present with any particular past," a bizarre notion that most physicists reject. Still, I should point out that although Bell's idea was bizarre, at least one science fiction writer thought of it long before Bell; see John Robinson Pierce's "Mr. Kinkaid's Pasts":

> There is no unique past! The uncertainty principle of Heisenberg, which philosophers use to assure us that the world is not a predestined machine, without room for free will, leading to one unique future, just as decisively contradicts the idea of a unique past . . . there is an infinity of pasts which are

consistent with all the evidences in our present universe, and any of these pasts is as much the real past as any other.

MULTIPLE TIME TRACKS AND PARALLEL WORLDS

Although most early time-travel analysts based their work on general relativity alone, many now think quantum mechanics has much to contribute as well. One analyst who holds this opinion is David Deutsch at the Oxford University (England) Mathematical Institute. Deutsch feels that general relativity is actually not the proper theory with which to study the physical effects of closed timelike lines in space-time (see his paper in the bibliography). He believes that the traditional mathematical machinery of general relativity actually obscures, not clarifies, the difficult task of separating the merely counterintuitive from the truly unphysical (and with time travel, there is plenty of both). Indeed, he calls the conventional space-time methods based on general relativity and differential geometry "perverse."

Deutsch also does not like the technical and conceptual problems of general relativity's wormholes and singularities. Deutsch says any nonquantum mechanical discussion concerning what he calls the "pathologies" of backward time travel is simply not adequate. In particular, Deutsch classifies these pathologies into two categories: (1) paradoxical constraints, e.g., the problem of free will in the grandfather paradox, and (2) causal loops that create information, e.g., a mathematician who is visited in his youth by a time traveler from the future (an older version of himself) who gives him the proof of a theorem for which the mathematician is (will be) famous in the future. So where did the proof come from—who actually thought of the proof?

Deutsch claims that his quantum mechanical analyses show the first class of pathologies simply does not occur (which I think is true). The past the time traveler enters is (according to Deutsch and in accordance with the theme of this chapter) not the past of the world the time traveler left, but the past of a parallel world. This view is old hat to science fiction, however. The first tale incorporating this idea appeared decades before either Everett or Deutsch thought on such matters. D.R. Daniels's "The Branches of Time" (*Wonder Stories*, August 1935) contains the telling observation that while splitting time tracks may allow individuals to change the past for the better (something, as Deutsch argues, that can't be done with just one time line), any such change is still futile in the end. As Daniels's time traveler puts it, sadly:

> I did have an idea to . . . go back to make past ages more liveable. Terrible things have happened in history, you know. But it isn't any use. Think, for instance, of the martyrs and the things they suffered. I could go back and save them those wrongs. And yet all time . . . they would still have known their unhappiness and their agony, because in this world-line those things happened. At the end, it's all unchangeable; it merely unrolls before us.

After Daniels's tale, the splitting time line concept quickly became part of standard science fiction lore, and writers could use it without having to offer a lot of explanation (and you can, too). For example, in J. MacCreigh's "A Hitch in Time" (*Thrilling Wonder Stories*, June 1947), the author didn't say much about his "First Law of Chronistics," which determines the development of "the branches of Fan-Shaped time." It was sufficient for his readers to understand, should a time traveler to the past change anything, this misstep would create a parallel branch of time on which the time traveler would be trapped; "The man who interfered with the space-time matrix, displacing even a comma in the great scroll of time, would be cut off from his origin forever."

Perhaps the best story of splitting time lines, which uses MacCreigh's idea of time-track trapping, is the 1953 novel by Ward Moore, *Bring the Jubilee*, in which Lee wins the Battle of Gettysburg (and the South wins the Civil War). Moore explores the implications of this historical deviation with the description of the invention of the HX-1, a time machine at the end. By using this time machine, a historian travels from 1952 into the past of 1863 to study the battle;

once there, he inadvertently disrupts events to the point that the North wins and reality splits, with the new fork in time representing the time track of our world. The historian is trapped on the new fork, cut off forever from his original track's future. The entire novel is in the form of a discovered manuscript, written in 1877 and found in 1953; the pathos of what must be the historian's ultimate isolation gives great emotional impact to the story.

A more recent novel on the same theme, Harry Turtledove's 1992 *The Guns of the South*, begins with a fascinating premise but completely misses the issue of single versus multiple time tracks. In this work, racists from the year 2014 arrive by time machine at Lee's 1864 winter camp. They bring with them AK-47 automatic rifles and offer to supply Lee's army with as many as it can use. Lee accepts and the South wins the Civil War. The future, of course, changes— or does it? The time travelers have also brought books from the future showing the South lost the war, implying that history must have forked. But all through the novel the time travelers move back and forth between the nineteenth and twenty-first centuries, apparently finding their own time unchanged. If that is true, the whole point of the story vanishes. It is an interesting book, well written, but in my humble opinion *Bring the Jubilee* is the superior work of science fiction.

A recent work that used the idea of splitting universes (called *multiplicity* in this story), and treated the physics honestly is Stephen Baxter's impressive 1995 novel *The Time Ships*. This tale, which tells the story of Wells's time traveler after the 1895 story ends, repeats the idea of becoming lost on an infinity of history-splitting time lines. Baxter poignantly expresses the emotional toll of this situation when the time traveler and his companion finally repair their damaged time machine after having been trapped fifty million years in the past. His friend asks the time traveler, "Where do you want to go?" and the reply is "Home. 1891." His friend explains, "It is lost in the Multiplicity." Baxter extends the splitting universe idea beyond what I've seen even the most speculative physicists do in scientific literature, and I strongly urge you to read this novel as an entertaining way to see how to properly handle the quantum mechanics of time travel.

Before returning to the quantum mechanical science of time travel, let me end this part of the discussion on splitting time tracks with a startling theological question recently raised by a philosopher. Arguing that God cannot branch along multiple time tracks (God is unique), the philosopher concludes that God must therefore exist in exactly *one* of how ever many different time tracks there may be. What if that chosen time track isn't ours? Might we then conclude that Nietzsche's nineteenth-century metaphorical claim that God is dead could be literally true? And how does God decide which new time track on which to exist each time a new temporal fork develops? Surely there is a good story in this somewhere.

CHRONOLOGY PROTECTION

So bizarre is the idea of time travel to the past that many physicists, whose bread-and-butter work is outrageous by most standards, still cannot bring themselves to accept time tripping. Such physicists think the "hard science" fiction writer Larry Niven is correct with his famous denial of time travel:

> Niven's Law: If the universe of discourse permits the possibility of time travel and of changing the past, then no time machine will be invented in that universe.

One physicist who thinks this right is Stephen Hawking, who in 1991 proposed his version of Niven's Law, calling it the *Chronology Protection Conjecture*. In fact, Hawking takes the position that his quantum analyses forbid the realization of any possible mechanism to implement time travel; he writes, "If you try to create a wormhole to use as a time machine, you have to warp the light cone structure of space-time so much that closed timelike curves appear anyway," making the specific details of a wormhole irrelevant. Hawking denies the creation of closed timelike curves by any means (wormholes, cosmic strings, rotating cylinders, whatever). Remember: A region of space-time containing closed timelike lines is said to be a time machine.

Hawking feels so strongly on this issue that he thinks Nature couldn't survive if time travel were possible. He believes his conjecture (which he has yet been unable to prove) "makes the universe safe for historians." Perhaps a fictional treatment of Hawking's concern is given in R.F. Jones's "Sunday Is Three Thousand Years Away" (*Thrilling Wonder Stories*, June 1950). In this story, a Master Historian and his students in a graduate course called "Experimental History," in the forty-sixth century, try to correct a problem created by previous tampering with the past.

Hawking's anecdotal evidence for his conjecture is so outrageous it is difficult to imagine that he really believes in its merit. As he writes in his 1993 collection (*Black Holes and Baby Universes and other essays*) about time travel, "The best evidence that time travel never will be possible is that we have not been invaded by hordes of tourists from the future." Never? I must admit I am puzzled by Hawking's fascination with this simplistic argument (the same argument he gave in 1991 when he originally put forth his conjecture); it is an argument that I don't think actually proves much of anything.

There is, in fact, one obvious rebuttal to Hawking's no-hordes-of-tourists argument, one that appeared in science fiction decades ago. As discussed in chapter nine, several very different mechanisms for time travel to the past have been invented (on paper), but they all share a common feature. In every case, you cannot travel back to a time before the date of the time machine's construction (neatly eliminating the paradox of a time traveler going back to tell himself how to make a time machine). That is, there are no hordes of tourists among us today because time travel hasn't been invented—yet. Oliver Saari explicitly states this idea in his story "The Time Bender" (*Astounding Stories*, August 1937), which uses a time machine based on warping space-time with a plate of superdense material (a form of the exotic matter mentioned in chapter nine). As the author explains, the time traveler "could not travel into the past, for the plate had to exist in all ages traveled, and it had not existed before he had made it." In the words of Frank Tipler (the discoverer of the rotating cylinder time machine), "Unless some really advanced beings have already made one of these things [a time machine, in the very distant past], we're not going back to visit the dinosaurs."

THE BACK REACTION

But that doesn't mean a time machine couldn't be built tomorrow, and in that case time travelers could begin to appear among us the day after tomorrow. And try as he might, Hawking has been unable to prove his conjecture, although he has attempted to do so by showing, at the quantum level (where quantum field fluctuations reach brief but enormous levels), the instability of the Cauchy horizon (see chapter nine again) due to the buildup of infinite stress-energies that literally tear space-time apart. This death-spasm is called the *back reaction*. It is an idea that has received very little treatment in the fictional literature. However, one story published three years before the announcement of Hawking's conjecture seems to have anticipated his position. Timothy Zahn's "Time Bomb" (*New Destinies*, Summer 1988) is filled with vivid descriptions of what seems (to me, anyway) to be quantum field back reactions resulting from multiple attempts to build a time machine. A much more recent story dealing specifically with back reaction effects is Paul Levinson's "The Chronology Protection Case" (*Analog*, September 1995).

Perhaps the best way to conclude this chapter is to quote a physicist who recently wrote, "Much investigation, both in the physics of quantum gravity and in the philosophy of reversibility, has to be carried out before one could have a clear sense of what exactly quantum gravity is trying to reveal about the secret of time." These are my sentiments, exactly. And it leaves a lot of flexibility for writers of time-travel fiction to exercise their imaginations.

SUMMARY

This chapter opened with the observation that general relativity (GR) is, today, not compatible with quantum mechanics (QM), so

GR cannot be the final theory of space-time (or of time travel). The amalgamation of GR and QM will give the theory of space-time, called *quantum gravity*. We defined the touchstone of QM, the *uncertainty principle*, and outlined its use in time travel fiction. The suggestion from today's understanding of QM, that a time traveler to the past could split the time track of the universe (and thereby avoid the problems of the paradoxes), was discussed. We emphasized this idea, the *many-worlds* interpretation of QM, and the distinction between it and yet another popular science fiction theme of *parallel worlds*. Using QM, Stephen Hawking has tried to prove his *chronology protection conjecture*, which says time travel to the past is impossible, but so far he has failed to prove it. He claims QM will introduce destructive space-time *back reaction* effects that will destroy any putative time machine before it can actually travel into the past, which is his explanation as to why we don't see "hordes of tourists" from the future among us today. We discussed the use of this idea in science fiction.

CHAPTER 12

Reading the Physics Literature for Story Ideas

If only he'd paid more attention to mathematics in school.

> regretful thought of Albert Eustace Rossi, the
> world's first time traveler, (in Damon Knight's
> "Extempore." (*Far Out* 1961).

A little mathematics never hurt a practical man. I was self-taught, and it slowed me down.

> Higgston Rainbird, inventor of the first time ma-
> chine, (in R.A. Lafferty's "Rainbird" (*Galaxy Science
> Fiction*, December 1961).

The best place to get state-of-the-art technical information concerning time travel and time machines, literally hot-off-the-press, is the scholarly physics literature. You do not have to be able to read every word in super-mathematical articles in exquisite detail. I won't be revealing any secrets here when I tell you that there are probably only a few dozen scientists world-wide who read any particular time machine article in complete detail and track through each and every differential-tensor equation with unrelenting patience. Many simply skim through such papers, looking for the flavor (if you will) of the physics. You can do the same, looking for story ideas (and at the end of this chapter I'll give you an example of one such idea to show you what you can expect to find).

Larry Niven, for example, found the title for his short story "Rotating Cylinders and the Possibility of Global Causality Violation" in scholarly literature. For this tale (which appeared in his 1979 collection *Convergent Series*), Niven used a Tipler cylinder (recall chapter nine) for his time machine, and in an introductory note he admits, "This story has a catchy title. I stole it from a mathematics paper by Frank J. Tipler." Niven tells us nothing more, but interested readers might want to look at the journal *Physical Review D* (No. 9, April 15, 1974, pp. 2203-2206).

Physical Review D is, in fact, probably the physics journal of greatest interest to the science fiction writer looking for time travel inspiration. (This journal publishes twice a month, on the first and the fifteenth, and the issue from the fifteenth you want—it carries articles devoted to "particles, fields, gravitation and cosmology.") Other journals, too, often publish time machine analyses. They include *Physical Review Letters*, *Physics Letters A*, *Physics Letters B*, *Classical and Quantum Gravity*, *Foundations of Physics*, *Nuclear Physics B*, *Il Nuovo Cimento B* (an Italian journal printed in English), and the *International Journal of Theoretical Physics*. Many of these journals are almost certainly in the physics collection of your local college or university. But what about all the journals your local library doesn't have? How do you search them for possible story ideas?

The answer is the one publication that every technical library is sure to have—*Physics Abstracts*. Twice a month, on the first and the fifteenth, *Physics Abstracts* prints the abstracts (a 150- to 200-word author-written prose summary of his or her paper) of 6,000 scholarly physics papers. You don't have to read all of them (thank God). To be sure you see all the latest time machine papers, simply skim through the two or three dozen (at most) abstracts listed in Section 4.00 for papers on relativity and gravitation. When you find something that looks interesting, you can go directly to the journal that published the paper, or order a photocopy of it through your local school's Inter-Library Loan service (see the opening discussion in the bibliography). I personally found *Physics Abstracts* to be absolutely essential when writing my book *Time Machines.*

Let me give you an example of a story idea you might expect to find in a search through the scholarly archives. The following is a concept I found in a wormhole time machine analysis by two Russian physicists (I.D. Novikov and A. Lossev), titled "The Jinn of the Time Machine; Nontrivial Self-Consistent Solutions" (*Classical and Quantum Gravity 9,* October 1992, pp. 2309-2321). As far as I know, nobody has done anything with it in a fictional context—yet. The authors begin by admitting that any wormhole, whether natural in origin or artificial (i.e., constructed by an "arbitrarily advanced civilization") will almost certainly not be anywhere near Earth. (A reasonable assumption—although the 1994 film *Stargate* takes the opposite view—given the volume of the solar system as compared to the volume of known space). The wormhole might, in fact, be in another galaxy. Even if it exists, it seems of no use to anybody on Earth at that distance.

In their paper, Lossev and Novikov suggest such a wormhole might actually be very useful, even if its location is completely unknown. Lossev and Novikov assume that the wormhole has existed as a time machine for a sufficiently long time (the significance will be clear by the end of the next several paragraphs). With that assumption, they make an information-creating time loop, the sort of thing so many science fiction writers have used to good effect for decades (but without any real scientific theory for support).

Lossev and Novikov begin their analysis by assuming that people have no knowledge of building a spacecraft to make the interstellar voyage to the distant wormhole, even if they knew which direction to go to reach the mouth that leads backward in time (call it mouth

B). So, they build an automatic spacecraft construction plant that can follow any detailed sequence of instructions provided, and they stockpile it with a supply of raw materials (energy, steel, plastic, computers, etc.). When the spacecraft construction is complete, the last step before launching the spacecraft toward mouth *B* will be to load the craft's on-board computer with the following three pieces of information:

a. the detailed sequence of instructions needed for the construction of the spacecraft

b. the direction from Earth to mouth *B*

c. the direction from mouth *A* (the wormhole exit mouth into the past) back to Earth.

So, people build the automatic plant, load it with raw materials, and then withdraw. This last step is crucial, as it eliminates human free will from further consideration; it removes any temptation to create a bilking paradox. What happens next?

Lossev and Novikov suggest that what happens next is quite dramatic—a very old spacecraft suddenly appears in the sky and lands next to the automatic construction plant. In its on-board computer are items *a*, *b* and *c*. Using item *a*, the automatic plant makes a new spacecraft, loads its new on-board computer with items *a*, *b* and *c* from the very old spacecraft's computer, and then the new spacecraft is launched toward mouth *B* (using the information of item *b*). The very old spacecraft is given an honored place in a museum.

Now, back to the new spacecraft, far out in space and racing into the future. Eventually, in the very far future, it arrives at the distant mouth *B*; it is now an old spacecraft (but not yet a *very* old one). It then plunges into mouth *B* and almost immediately emerges from mouth *A*, into the past. Indeed, it repeats this process (items *b* and *c* are sufficient to determine how to travel from mouth *A* back to mouth *B*) as many times as required until it is in the far-distant past, at a time even before it left Earth. Specifically, the spacecraft repeatedly uses the wormhole time machine until it is far enough in the past that it can cruise back to Earth at normal speed (it knows the way back because of item *c*) and arrive as a very old spacecraft, just in time to be placed in the museum. (Now you know the meaning of the requirement that the wormhole time machine have existed for a "sufficiently long time," i.e., long enough to make this entire process possible. Remember that a wormhole cannot be used as a time machine to travel back before it was a time machine.)

As Lossev and Novikov point out, this remarkable closed sequence of consistent events has increased knowledge from what it was at the time just before the automatic plant was built. People now know how to build an interstellar spacecraft and the locations of both mouths of the wormhole. They also now possess a very old, used spacecraft. It is curious to note that while the information in the spacecraft's computer memory has traveled on a closed time loop, the spacecraft itself has not. This is because the spacecraft left Earth when new but arrived back (before it left) very old, whereupon it promptly entered a museum. There is, therefore, no question about the origin of the very old spacecraft. Where did the information of items *a*, *b* and *c* come from? Lossev and Novikov say it came from the energy gained by the spacecraft as it interacted (will interact?) with the rest of the universe while on its wonderful journey.

Now, that's a great concept. There could be a great story in there just waiting for somebody to work it into shape. Why don't *you* try your hand at it?

GLOSSARY OF SELECTED TERMS AND CONCEPTS

advanced solution: the prediction by Maxwell's electromagnetic field equations of radio waves that travel into the past (see also *Dirac radio*).

antimatter: quantum mechanical prediction (verified experimentally) that all fundamental particles of matter come in two versions (the *normal* version and the *antimatter* version). The positron, for example, is the antiparticle version of the electron, differing only in the sign of its electric charge. The photon, on the other hand, is its own antiparticle. An antiparticle traveling forward in time can be thought of as its *normal* version traveling backwards in time.

arrow of time: the statement that time appears to have a direction. There are several different arrows; the psychological (we remember the past, we anticipate the future), the thermodynamic (organized systems evolve toward disorganization), the electromagnetic (radio waves propagate away from their sources) and the cosmological (the expansion of the universe is directed toward the future).

back reaction: the tendency of space-time to resist the formation of closed timelike lines.

Big Bang: the singular beginning of space-time, generally thought of as a gigantic explosion.

bilking paradox: caused by disrupting a causal loop. For example, suppose a time traveler builds a time machine using plans he received years earlier from a mysterious stranger. He now realizes that the stranger was himself, using the time machine to travel back into the past to give his younger self the plans (see *causal loop*). A bilking paradox is created if the time traveler builds the time machine, verifies that it works, and then decides *not* to visit his younger-self to hand over the plans.

black hole: a region of space-time where gravity is so strong that nothing can escape, including light. Black holes are formed when sufficiently massive stars burn-out. A black hole of ten solar masses would have a radius of about twenty miles. Black holes might also have been created at the Big Bang and, if so, they theoretically could come in any mass and size; a black hole with the mass of the Earth would have a diameter of less than half an inch.

block universe: a space-time in which all world-lines are completely
   determined, from beginning to end (a fatalistic universe).
Cauchy horizon: the (hyper)surface in space-time that marks the transition
   from predictability to unpredictability of the behavior (in time) of a system
   (see *chronology horizon*).
causal loop: a time loop containing an event caused by a *later* event which,
   itself, is caused by the earlier event (see the example in *bilking paradox*).
causality: the claim that every event is caused by a prior event. Time travel
   to the past inherently violates causality.
chronology horizon: the (hyper)surface in space-time separating a region
   containing closed timelike lines (sometimes called a *dischronal* region)
   from the rest of space-time which does not contain such time machine/
   time travel world-lines. A chronology horizon is a special case of the more
   general Cauchy horizon.
chronology protection: the claim that time machines and time travel to the past
   are impossible because of the back reaction (popularized among physicists
   as the *Hawking chronology protection conjecture*, but it was stated earlier by
   science fiction writer Larry Niven).
closed timelike line (or curve): a timelike world-line of finite length that has
   no ends, i.e., that forms a closed loop in space-time. A region of space-time
   containing closed timelike lines is said to be a time machine.
conservation law: physical quantities in interacting systems that remain
   unchanged are said to be conserved. Total energy and total momentum
   (linear and angular) are conserved quantities.
cosmic string: hypothetical, threadlike space-time structures with enormous
   mass-energy (and density) that may have been formed during the Big
   Bang. Cosmic strings do not violate the weak energy condition (as do
   wormholes), and theoretically they can create closed timelike lines.
cosmological constant: an extra term added by Einstein to the general theory
   of relativity specifically to keep that theory from predicting the expansion
   of the universe (which was later observationally confirmed). Einstein later
   said it was the greatest mistake of his life. The constant (which is today
   believed to be almost zero, if not zero) appears in Gödel's rotating time
   travel space-time as a determining factor in the minimum radius of a closed
   timelike line.

determinism: the belief that effects are uniquely determined by causes.

Dirac radio: science fiction gadget for sending signals at infinite speed, which thus travel backward in time (see also *ultraluminal*).

electron: fundamental particle of mass (carrying one quantum of negative electric charge) that orbits the nuclei of atoms and plays a central role in determining the chemical properties of the elements and their compounds.

Else-When: the collection of space-time events that cannot be reached from the Here-Now with a timelike line.

entropy: a measure of the randomness of a system. Entropy plays the central role in the thermodynamic arrow of time.

ether: a substance once thought to fill all of space to allow radiation something to propagate through (as opposed to simply a vacuum). The special theory of relativity showed ether was an unnecessary concept because it has no observable effects (physicists argue that if something is impossible to detect, it is meaningless to talk about it as being part of science).

event: a point in space-time.

event horizon: the space-time surface of a black hole, at which light can just escape to the outside universe. It is called a horizon because, by definition, an external observer can't see beyond it and into the interior of the black hole. To see the inside of a black hole you must enter the hole (but then you can't get out).

exotic matter: matter that violates one or both of the energy conditions (weak/strong).

fourth dimension: either time or a fourth spatial dimension.

frame of reference: a space-time coordinate system.

free will: the belief that we can choose to do what we do. There is no free will in a block universe.

future: the collection of space-time events that can be reached from the Here-Now via a timelike line directed toward a later time (for each individual, what hasn't yet been experienced).

gamma ray: very high energy, very high frequency electro-magnetic radiation. Gamma rays have frequencies on the order of ten trillion times greater than those of AM broadcast radio waves.

general theory of relativity: Einstein's theory of curved space-time that explains gravity in terms of nothing but geometry. Its fundamental premise is that all the laws of physics should appear the same to all observers in any reference frame. It is believed the theory will fail when the local mass-energy density reaches a level of about 10^{58} grams/cm^3, a density so enormous (the density of water is just 1 gram/cm^3) that there is no known mechanism for achieving it anywhere in the universe other than in another Big Bang.

geodesic: the shortest path connecting two points in a space.

global: in the large.

Gödel universe: a space-time that is rotating (unlike the one we live in) so fast that it automatically generates closed timelike lines; in such a universe, time travel to the past would be a natural phenomenon.

grandfather paradox: classic time-travel paradox, in which a time traveler, while at a date in the past before his conception, kills an ancestor directly linked to the birth of the time traveler. A time traveler simply killing his own younger self is a more direct form of this type of paradox.

Hawking radiation: the emission of particles (energy) by a black hole from outside its event horizon, resulting in the eventual evaporation of the hole. This is a quantum mechanical effect.

Here-Now: the point or event in space-time that separates the past, the future and Else-When.

hyperspace: a space of four or more dimensions (four-dimensional space-time is a hyperspace).

inertial frame: any frame of reference in which Newton's laws of mechanics are true (there is no relative acceleration between inertial frames, so a rotating or "merry-go-round" frame is not inertial).

invariance: a quantity that remains the same in any frame of reference is an invariant; e.g., the distance between any two points on a piece of paper is independent of any particular coordinate system, and the speed of light is the same for all observers.

Kerr black hole: a rotating black hole.

light cone: the lightlike surface in space-time that, at each point in space-time, separates the past from the future from Else-When.

lightlike: the world-line of a photon (or of any other form of mass-energy traveling at the speed of light).

local: in the small.

Lorentz factor: the ubiquitous square-root expression that appears in many relativistic calculations, such as time dilation, length contraction, and the variation of mass with speed. For example, the mass, m, of a moving body is not independent of its speed v, but rather varies as

$$m = \frac{m_0}{\sqrt{1 - (v/c)^2}},$$

where m_0 is the rest mass (that is, the mass when $v = 0$) and c denotes the speed of light (186,200 miles per second). The denominator is the Lorentz factor.

Lorentz-FitzGerald contraction: the conclusion from special relativity that the appearance (to a stationary observer) of a moving object will be shortened in length along the direction of motion. (Many years after Einstein's work, it was shown that the object will also appear to be rotated.)

many-worlds interpretation: quantum mechanical view of splitting universes.

mass-energy: The famous $E = mc^2$, the equation behind nuclear fission and fusion weapons.

mind travel: time travel of the consciousness without being accompanied by the body or any other physical artifact.

Minkowski space-time: the flat space-time of the special theory of relativity. There is no gravity, and no time travel, in this space-time.

non-Euclidean geometry: the geometry of space-time, whether curved or flat. Space-time is nonintuitive precisely because it is always hard to resist thinking in terms of high school Euclidean geometry, which is simply the wrong geometry.

observer: physicist lingo for somebody equipped with recording instruments (e.g., a clock, a notepad, etc.)

parallel worlds: simultaneous existence of multiple (perhaps infinite) versions of reality in hyperspace.

past: the collection of space-time events that can reach the Here-Now via a timelike line directed from an earlier time (for each individual, what has already been experienced).

photon: the particle of light.

Planck length: the shortest nonzero length in quantum theory (about 10^{-34} centimeters).

proper time: the time-keeping of an observer's clock.

pulps: the old science fiction magazines, through the 1940s (published on inexpensive, wood pulp paper).

quantized energy: energy that is constrained to change in steps, not smoothly and continuously, from one value to another value. An example is the energy levels of electrons in an atom. The quantum of energy is the step size, which for atoms is very, very tiny (and this is why we don't notice the granular nature of quantized energy in our everyday lives).

quantum gravity: the yet-to-be-discovered theory that combines quantum mechanics with general relativity.

quantum mechanics: the exact physics of the very small (i.e., atoms and smaller).

quantum theory: any theory in which physical quantities are not continuous, but rather assume their values in discrete jumps (the size of the jump is the *quantum*).

recurrence paradox: the theory that every system will return to every previous state infinitely often if you wait long enough.

reinterpretation principle: asserts that negative mass-energy traveling forward in time is positive mass-energy traveling backward in time (and vice versa).

reversibility paradox: the equations of physics contain no arrow of time; i.e., they work equally well with time running forward or backward (see also *advanced solution*).

Schwarzschild black hole: a spherically symmetric, nonrotating black hole.

self-consistency: the assertion that events on a closed timelike line must never be in contradiction.

sexual paradox: a special type of causal loop, where the connected events on a time loop are coupled (pun intended) through sex, e.g., a time traveler to the past who becomes his own ancestor.

singularity: a region in space-time where the curvature becomes infinite and the laws of physics fail. The Big Bang was a singularity, as is the center of a black hole—in a Schwarzschild black hole the singularity is a point, while in a Kerr black hole it is an extended region in the form of a ring.

spacelike: a world-line on which propagating mass-energy exceeds the speed of light.

space-time: the stuff out of which reality is built. Everything there is, the universe, is the total collection of events in space-time.

special theory of relativity: Einstein's theory of flat space-time, which assumes gravity doesn't exist (gravity is the result of the geometry of *curved* space-time). Its fundamental premise is that the laws of physics should appear the same to observers in different inertial frames.

splitting universes: the idea that every decision causes reality to split into separate copies, identical in every respect except for each of the different possible results of the decision.

stargate: science fiction name for the mouth of a wormhole.

strong energy condition: gravity is always attractive. Wormholes violate this condition.

subluminal: slower than light.

superluminal: faster than light.

tachyon: a particle (hypothetical, so far) that always travels faster than light (its world line is spacelike).

tensor: mathematical generalization of the vector concept. Einstein's gravitational field equations are tensor-differential equations (e.g., the metric tensor contains information about the curvature of space-time), while Newton's and Maxwell's equations are simpler, vector-differential equations.

tidal force: force experienced by a nonpoint mass (one with spatial extension) in a non-uniform gravitational field. Such forces tend to simultaneously compress and stretch extended masses. Black holes and wormhole mouths can generate enormous tidal forces on extended masses no larger than a human body. Interestingly, the more massive a black hole is the less severe are its tidal forces at distances outside the event horizon. However, no matter what the black hole mass, the tidal forces are infinite at the central singularity.

time dilation: the slowing of the rate of time-keeping by a clock, either by motion or by gravity.

timelike: a world-line on which propagating mass-energy always travels slower than light.

time police: story characters in science fiction charged with preventing time travelers from changing the past.

timewarp: science fiction name for a time machine.

Tipler cylinder: infinitely long cylinder, made of exotic matter, rotating so fast
   around its long axis that it warps space-time enough to create closed
   timelike lines that encircle the cylinder. Can be used as a time machine to
   travel both into the future and the past (but not to a time before the creation
   of the cylinder).

twin paradox: the conclusion from special relativity that a clock's rate of time-
   keeping slows with motion.

ultraluminal: motion sufficiently superluminal that mass-energy appears to
   travel backwards in time (see also *Dirac radio*).

uncertainty principle: the statement in quantum mechanics that says certain
   pairs of quantities cannot be simultaneously measured with arbitrarily small
   error. Location and momentum, and energy and time, are two such pairs.

wave function: mathematical entity in quantum mechanics that measures a
   system's probability of being in any particular state.

weak energy condition: observed mass-energy density at every point in space-
   time is always non-negative for every observer on a timelike world-line.
   Quantum mechanics predicts (and it has been experimentally confirmed)
   that there are exceptions.

white dwarf: a burnt-out star with less than 1.4 solar masses, of planetary size.
   The ultimate fate of our sun.

world-line: the trajectory of mass-energy in space-time.

wormhole: a space-time structure (violating both energy conditions, weak and
   strong) connecting two points of the same space-time (or even two *different*
   space-times, i.e., two different universes) with a timelike path requiring
   less travel time than does a photon traveling between the two points outside
   of the wormhole. Can be made into a time machine by creating a time shift
   (using time dilation) between the two mouths of the wormhole.

BIBLIOGRAPHY

BOOKS

One way to learn how to write good time travel science fiction is to study the works of excellent writers who have already created such tales. The titles that follow, containing many of the short stories discussed in this book, are available at most public libraries. If you can't find one or more of them at your local library, try the Inter-Library Loan Department at a nearby college or university. Schools will often provide their nationwide search-and-borrow services to local residents for a nominal fee (certainly nominal compared to the expense of attempting to buy an out-of-print book through a commercial finder).

An absolutely wonderful guide to all of early science fiction, up to 1930, with brief summaries of over 3,000 stories (including the very earliest time travel tales), is Everett F. Bleiler's *Science-Fiction, The Early Years* (Kent State University Press, 1990). You should be able to find it in the Reference Department of any good college library. An extensive bibliography to the modern time travel literature (including nonfictional works) can be found in my book *Time Machines*.

The Air of Mars. Edited by M. Ginsburg. New York: Macmillan, 1976.

The Arbor House Treasury of Great Science Fiction Short Novels. New York: Arbor House, 1980.

Australian Science Fiction. Edited by V. Ikin. Chicago: Academy Chicago, 1984.

Before the Golden Age (Volumes I, II and III). Edited by I. Asimov. New York: Doubleday, 1974.

The Best of Murray Leinster. Edited by B. Davis. London: Corgi, 1976.

The Best from Orbit. Edited by D. Knight. New York: Berkley, 1975.

The Best from the Rest of the World. Edited by D.A. Wollheim. Garden City, New York: Doubleday, 1976.

The Best of Science Fiction. Edited by G. Conklin. New York: Crown, 1946.

Beyond Time. Edited by S. Ley. New York: Pocket, 1976.

Beyond Time and Space. Edited by A. Derleth. New York: Pellegrini and Cudahy, 1950.

Coming Attractions. Edited by M. Greenberg. New York: Gnome, 1957.

The Classic Book of Science Fiction. Edited by G. Conklin. New York: Bonanza, 1982.

Criminal Justice Through Science Fiction. Edited by J.D. Olander and M.H. Greenberg. New York: New Viewpoints, 1977.

De Camp, L. Sprague. *Rivers of Time.* New York: Baen, 1993.

Dinosaur Fantastic. Edited by M. Resnik and M.H. Greenberg. New York: DAW, 1993.

Dinosaurs! Edited by J. Dann and G. Dozois. New York: Ace, 1990.

Epoch. Edited by R. Silverberg and R. Elwood. New York: Berkley, 1975.

The Expert Dreamers. Edited by F. Pohl. Garden City, New York: Doubleday, 1962.

The Fantastic Civil War. Edited by F. McSherry, Jr. New York: Baen, 1991.

Famous Science Fiction Stories. Edited by R.J. Healy and J.F. McComas. New York: Random House, 1957.

The Far Side of Time. Edited by R. Elwood. New York: Dodd, Mead, 1974.

Farley, R.M. *The Omnibus of Time.* Los Angeles: Fantasy Publishing, 1950.

Faster Than Light. Edited by J. Dann and G. Zebrowski. New York: Harper & Row, 1976.

Fifty Short Science Fiction Tales. Edited by I. Asimov and G. Conklin. New York: Macmillan, 1976.

Finney, Jack. *About Time.* New York: Simon and Schuster, 1986.

Great Science Fiction by Scientists. Edited by G. Conklin. New York: Collier, 1962.

Great Science Fiction Stories by the World's Great Scientists. Edited by I. Asimov, M.H. Greenberg and C.G. Waugh. New York: Donald I. Fine, 1985.

Great Stories of Science Fiction. Edited by M. Leinster. New York: Random House, 1955.

Last Door to Aiya. Edited by M. Ginsburg. New York: S.G. Phillips, 1968.

The Last Man on Earth. Edited by I. Asimov, M. Greenberg and C. Waugh. New York: Ballantine, 1982.

Microcosmic Tales. Edited by I. Asimov, M. Greenberg and J. Olander. New York: Taplinger, 1980.

The Mirror of Infinity. Edited by R. Silverberg. San Francisco: Canfield, 1970.

My Best Science Fiction Story. Edited by L. Margulies and O.J. Friend. New York: Merlin, 1949.

Nahin, P.J. *Time Machines: Time Travel in Physics, Metaphysics, and Science Fiction*. New York: American Institute of Physics, 1993 (corrected paperback reprint 1994).

New Worlds of Fantasy. Edited by T. Carr. New York: Ace, 1967.

Omnibus of Science Fiction. Edited by G. Conklin. New York: Crown, 1952.

One Hundred and One Science Fiction Stories. Edited by M. Greenberg and C. Waugh. New York: Avenel, 1986.

100 Great Science Fiction Short Stories. Edited by I. Asimov, M. Greenberg and J. Olander. New York: Avon, 1978.

The Other Worlds. Edited by P. Stong. Garden City, New York: Garden City Publishing, 1941.

The Penguin World Omnibus of Science Fiction. Edited by B. Aldiss and S.J. Lundwall. Middlesex: Penguin, 1986.

Pre-Revolutionary Russian Science Fiction. Edited by L. Fetzer. Ann Arbor, Michigan: Ardis, 1982.

Prize Science Fiction. Edited by D.A. Wollheim. New York: McBride, 1953.

Science-Fiction Adventures in Dimension. Edited by G. Conklin. New York: Vanguard, 1953.

Science Fiction of the 30's. Edited by D. Knight. New York: Avon, 1975.

Science Fiction of the 40's. Edited by F. Pohl. New York: Avon, 1978.

The Science Fictional Dinosaur. Edited by R. Silverberg, C. Waugh and M. Greenberg. New York: Avon, 1982.

Starships. Edited by I. Asimov, M.H. Greenberg and C.G. Waugh. New York: Ballantine, 1983.

Tales Out of Time. Edited by B. Ireson. New York: Philomel, 1981.

The Time Curve. Edited by S. Moskowitz and R. Elwood. New York: Tower, 1968.

Time Travelers. Edited by G. Dozois. New York: Ace, 1989.

The Time Travelers. Edited by R. Silverberg and M.H. Greenberg. New York: Primus, 1985.

Time Wars. Edited by C. Waugh and M.H. Greenberg. New York: Tor, 1986.

The Traps of Time. Edited by M. Moorcock. Middlesex: Penguin, 1970.

Treasury of Science Fiction. Edited by G. Conklin. New York: Bonanza, 1980.

Voyagers in Time. Edited by R. Silverberg. New York: Meredith Press, 1967.

What Might Have Been. Edited by G. Benford and M.H. Greenberg. New York: Bantam, 1989.

Worlds of Tomorrow. Edited by A. Derleth. New York: Pellegrini & Cudahy, 1953.

ARTICLES

The following is a list of nonfiction essays (pro and con) on time travel and related issues that are fairly accessible. With few exceptions, they require no special knowledge of physics or mathematics, and all are written in a stimulating manner. They will definitely make you think.

Asimov, I. "Faster Than Light," *Asimov's Science Fiction Magazine*, November 1984.

——"Time Travel," *Asimov's Science Fiction Magazine*, April 1984.

Blatt, J.M. "Time Reversal," *Scientific American*, August 1956.

Chown, M. "Planes, Trains and Wormholes," *New Scientist*, March 23, 1996.

Cramer, J.G. "Quantum Time Travel," *Analog*, April 1991.

——"Natural Wormholes: Squeezing the Vacuum," *Analog*, July 1992.

Deser, S., and R., Jakiw, "Time Travel?" *Comments on Nuclear and Particle Physics* 20 (September 1992): 337–354.

Deutsch, D., and M. Lockwood, "The Quantum Physics of Time Travel," *Scientific American*, March 1994.

Donaldson, T. "The Holes of Space-Time," *Analog*, July 1993.

L. Dwyer, "Time Travel and Some Alleged Logical Asymmetries Between Past and Future," *Canadian Journal of Philosophy* 8 (March 1978): 15–38.

——"How to Affect, But Not Change, the Past," *Southern Journal of Philosophy* 15 (1977): 383–385.

——"Time Travel and Changing the Past," *Philosophical Studies* 27 (May 1975): 341–350.

Einstein, A. "On the Generalized Theory of Gravitation," *Scientific American*, April 1950.

Faye, J. "The Past Revisited," *Danish Yearbook of Philosophy* 1987.

Fitzgerald, P. "Tachyons, Backwards Causation, and Freedom," *Boston Studies in the Philosophy of Science* 8 (1970): 415–436.

Forward, R. "How to Build a Time Machine," *Omni*, May 1980.

Fröman, P.O. "Historical Background of the Tachyon Concept," *Archive for History of Exact Sciences* 48 (1994): 373–380.

Fulmer, G. "Understanding Time Travel," *Southwestern Journal of Philosophy* 11 (Spring 1980): 151–156.

Gallois, A. "Asymmetry in Attitudes and the Nature of Time," *Philosophical Studies* 76 (October 1994): 51–69.

Godfrey-Smith, W. "Traveling in Time," *Analysis* 40 (March 1980): 72–73.

Gorovitz, S. "Leaving the Past Alone," *Philosophical Review* 73 (July 1964): 360–371.

Gould, J.D. "Hypothetical History," *Economic History Review* 22 (1969): 195–207.

Gribbin, J. "Granny Is Safe in the Past," *New Scientist*, August 12, 1995.

Harrison, J. "Jocasta's Crime," *Analysis* 39 (March 1979): 65.

Horwich, P. "On Some Alleged Paradoxes of Time Travel," *Journal of Philosophy* 72 (14 August 1975): 432–444.

Lafleur, L.J. "Marvelous Voyages - H.G. Wells' *The Time Machine*," *Popular Astronomy*, October 1943.

Lem, S. "The Time-Travel Story and Related Matters of SF Structuring," *Science-Fiction Studies* 1 (Spring 1974): 143–154.

Lewis, D. "The Paradoxes of Time Travel," *American Philosophical Quarterly* 13 (April 1976): 145–152.

MacBeath, M. "Who Was Dr. Who's Father?" *Synthese* 56 (July 1982): 397–430.

Malament, D.B. "Time Travel' in the Gödel Universe," *Proceedings of the Philosophy of Science Association* 2 (1984): 91–100.

Mavrodes, G.I. "Is the Past Unpreventable?" *Faith and Philosophy* 1 (April 1984): 131–146.

Nerlich, G. "Can Time Be Finite?" *Pacific Philosophical Quarterly* 62 (July 1981): 227–239.

Price, H. "The Philosophy and Physics of Changing the Past," *Synthese* 61 (December 1984): 299–323.

Purtill, R.L. "Foreknowledge and Fatalism," *Religious Studies* 10 (September 1974): 319–324.

Remnant, P. "Peter Damian: Could God Change the Past?" *Canadian Journal of Philosophy* 8 (June 1978): 259–268.

Schild, A. "Time," *Texas Quarterly* 3 (Autumn 1960): 42–62.

Smart, J.J.C. "Is Time Travel Possible?" *Journal of Philosophy* 60 (April 1963): 237–241.

Sorenson, R.A. "Time Travel, Parahistory and Hume," *Philosophy* 62 (April 1987): 227–236.

Spellman, L. "Causing Yesterday's Effects," *Canadian Journal of Philosophy* 12 (March 1982): 145–161.

Stewart, I. "The Real Physics of Time Travel," *Analog*, January 1994.

Swinburne, R.G. "Affecting the Past," *Philosophical Quarterly* 16 (October 1966): 341–347.

Thom, R. "Time Travel and Non-Fatal Suicide," *Philosophical Studies* 27 (March 1975): 211–216.

Travis, J. "Could a Pair of Cosmic Strings Open a Route Into the Past?" *Science*, April 10, 1992.

Vihvelin, K. "What Time Travelers Cannot Do," *Philosophical Studies* 81 (March 1996): 315–330.

Wachhorst, W. "Time-Travel Romance on Film: Archetypes and Structures," *Extrapolation* 25 (Winter 1984): 340–359.

Webb, C.W. "Could Time Flow? If So, How Fast?" *Journal of Philosophy* 57 (26 May 1960): 357–365.

Weingard, R. "Some Philosophical Aspects of Black Holes," *Synthese* 42 (September 1979): 191–219.

——"General Relativity and the Conceivability of Time Travel," *Philosophy of Science* 46 (June 1979): 328–332.

——"On Travelling Backward in Time," *Synthese* 24 (1972): 117–132.

Wheeler, J.A. "The Lesson of the Black Hole," *Proceedings of the American Philosophical Society* 125 (February 1981): 25–37.

Wheeler, J.C. "Of Wormholes, Time Machines, and Paradoxes," *Astronomy* (February 1996): 52–57.

Williams, D.C. "The Myth of Passage," *Journal of Philosophy* 48 (July 1951): 457–472.

Zetterberg, J.P. "Letting the Past Be Brought About," *Southern Journal of Philosophy* 17 (1979): 413–421.

Zwart, P.J. "The Flow of Time," *Synthese* 24 (1972): 133–158.

INDEX